One Place de l'Eglise

The library is always open at
renfrewshirelibraries.co.uk

Visit now for library news and
information,
to **renew and
reserve** online, and
to download
free eBooks.

Phone: 0300 300 1188
Email: libraries@renfrewshire.gov.uk

One Place de l'Eglise

A Year or Two in a French Village

TREVOR DOLBY

MICHAEL  JOSEPH

MICHAEL JOSEPH

UK | USA | Canada | Ireland | Australia
India | New Zealand | South Africa

Michael Joseph is part of the Penguin Random House group of companies
whose addresses can be found at global.penguinrandomhouse.com

Penguin
Random House
UK

First published 2022
001

Copyright © Trevor Dolby, 2022

The moral right of the author has been asserted

'Obituary of Jock Murray, copyright © The Estate of Patrick Leigh Fermor 2022.'
'Le coup de bélier dans les "piles" de Causses-et-Veyran', *Bulletin de la Société
archéologique, scientifique et littéraire de Béziers*, 2011–12, pp. 11–20.

Set in 13.5/16pt Garamond MT Std
Typeset by Jouve (UK), Milton Keynes
Printed and bound in Great Britain by Clays Ltd, Elcograf S.p.A.

The authorized representative in the EEA is Penguin Random House Ireland,
Morrison Chambers, 32 Nassau Street, Dublin D02 YH68

A CIP catalogue record for this book is available from the British Library

ISBN: 978–0–241–55632–0

www.greenpenguin.co.uk

To Kaz and Freya and George

Reader, you have here an honest book . . . in writing it, I have proposed to myself no other than a domestic and private end. I have had no consideration at all either to your service or to my glory . . . Thus, reader, I myself am the matter of my book: there's no reason that you should employ your leisure upon so frivolous and vain a subject.

> Michel Eyquem de Montaigne, *Essais: A Collection of Musings on Just About Anything* (1580)

What you keep for yourself, you lose. What you give away, you keep forever.

> Axel Munthe, *The Story of San Michele* (1929)

Nobody can be uncheered with a balloon.

> *Winnie-the-Pooh*

One Place de l'Eglise lies at the centre of the medieval village of Causses-et-Veyran (pronounced cause-A-vair-on) in the Languedoc, now officially called Occitanie. The village sits on the southern edge of the Causses, a series of limestone plateaus that extends into the Massif Central. Veyran is a derivative of the name of a Roman centurion whose villa was located nearby.

The Seventh Roman Legion was based in Béziers, 30 kilometres south, near the Mediterranean coast. A centurion's pension often included a piece of land, local to their garrison, on which they could build a home and retire in style. Many villages in the Languedoc with a name ending in 'an' (or sometimes 'ac') are villages built around a retired centurion's villa.

There are 5,769 villages in France with a 'Place de l'Eglise', making it the second most popular street name in France. It is pipped to the top spot by its sibling Rue de l'Eglise, at 7,965. One day I would like to invite all those who live in a 1 Place de l'Eglise to a big fête with T-shirts, *traiteur* and tintinnabulation . . .

Contents

Things We Might Want to Know More of

Four innocents – a reluctant bar owner – an open secret – a butcher – catering for 500 – fisticuffs in the Place du Marché

It was the night of the Fête. I was chatting to Dido in the Place du Marché when the fight broke out. It was a rip-roaring saloon-bar special.

Dido was happy to have a new ear to bend. She had never meant to run the village bar. It was the *maire* and a couple of others who had cajoled her into the act of madness that had ruined her life. 'I'm an artist,' she told me loudly. 'I get up at seven to the sound of banging on the door for coffee. I close at midnight with the same people not wanting to go home. I mean, what was it, *une maison close*? Anyone would have a nervous breakdown, and I certainly did and I've no intention of opening again until Monsieur-le-Maire repays me the fortune I spent doing up the place.' Did I know how much time she had spent? Did I know how selfish people were? Did I know of anyone who would like to take it off her hands for a reasonable price and allow her to up sticks to Paris, where her real destiny lay at Place du Tertre or Pigalle? 'Ha!' she blurted and stormed off, arms to the sky.

Marie-Claire sat on her chair next to where we stood. Marie-Claire was our eighty-plus-year-old next-door neighbour and our first friend in the village. It seemed to me she spoke French the way I speak French: with no discernible sense or purpose. Every utterance is a commitment to optimism and faith. Largely inaudible and sometimes as if I'm just pulling random clicks and whistles from my mind, sounds find their way to my mouth in the hope that they might miraculously of their own accord form a French sentence that someone will understand. My French is a living linguistic experiment. If one day I can speak the language with any degree of fluency, the feat will prove beyond doubt that the world is flat and precisely 6,026 years old.

Marie-Claire was a burglar. Not long after we arrived that first summer holiday, I said to Hans and Lotten Bjerke – Swedes who speak better English than I do – who live opposite us, what a nice old lady Marie-Claire was. Hans rocked back on his Swedish brogues and whispered that I should keep my door closed, as she was wont to pop in and borrow things. Well, that's all right, I said, 'borrow' being the word I latched on to. 'No! Not all right!' he announced and proceeded to tell me that Marie-Claire pops in to borrow things like ornaments, pots, pans, kitchen condiments such as the odd gallon of good olive oil, plants, cutlery, portable tools such as screwdrivers and hammers, books, small electronic equipment and perishables in the form of food from the fridge. Apparently the locals nipped into her house now and again when she was wandering the village and repatriated their goods. Marie-Claire didn't seem to mind and merely commenced collecting all over again.

I nodded *bonjour* to her and signalled to my family I was off to get us all another drink. I wove my way to the temporary 30-metre-long bar, not unlike those I'm told you find in dusty outback Australian rugby clubs, and bought two plastic beakers of Muscat and a couple of Cokes. Four drinks clasped in two hands, I tottered through the milling stragglers who had not yet taken their seats and for the fourth time was asked by one of the young village girls if I was eating. I said no, and she shrugged and went on her way hustling – or trying to hustle – people to their places. I handed a Muscat to my wife and the Cokes to my children.

'Well,' I said jovially, 'I told you this would be fun.'

'It's hot,' said Kaz.

'Well, it's fun. I wouldn't exactly say hot.'

'Don't be an arse. The temperature. I'm broiling here.'

It had been around 37 degrees all day, and the temperature was still around 32. Everyone in the square was red-faced and dripping. I took a sip of the sweet, warm, local hooch then from behind me I heard a shout.

'*B-b-bon-j-jour*, M-m-m-madame Dolby!' I turned to find our stuttering, hirsute, pocket-battleship of a butcher striding towards us, arms outstretched, dark-blue cheeks and chin where he had shaved ten minutes previously with a Laguiole and which had already grown back. He must be swilling with testosterone. I bet he could inseminate a wild boar from twenty paces by just looking at it. I like Monsieur le Butcher (liked, I should say, I didn't yet know there was a dark side to him). I can understand him. By the time he has uttered a sentence I have had time to look up every word in a dictionary, compose a response and choose my evening meal for the next three weeks. Monsieur le Butcher has, like everyone else in the village, at least three jobs. On the one hand he runs the butcher's shop; his meat – never displayed out front, always concealed in the huge walk-in fridge – competes favourably with anything a Soho-butcher-to-the-stars can muster. He seems to have every cut from nose to tail and in any style or form. I swear he manicures his trotters before he wraps them. At Christmas the panoply of produce is mind-boggling. There are local oysters, langoustines, sea bass, white fish of every type, cheeses, every type of fowl you can think of: snipe, quail, duck, pigeon, woodcock and, as a nod to the culinarily uneducated, turkey and chicken. Monsieur le Butcher also runs his own restaurant in the next village up in the mountains, where the speciality is cow's hoof. And, to boot, he also caters at fêtes.

Monsieur le Butcher shook my hand with enthusiasm, kissed Kaz – left, right, left – gestured to my children, George and Freya, and, by whistling through his teeth and raising the flat of his hand, indicated their vast height (neither was then over 1.6 metres tall). He continued in sign language, which will not be appearing on a daytime TV programme for the deaf any time soon, to suggest how clever I had been creating two such huge and healthy children. He shook my hand vigorously again. It was going to be a good night, he said, rubbing his palms together. By this time vans of victuals were arriving, and Monsieur le Butcher indicated that he was organizing the food and had duties to perform, so off he went smiling through the throng.

The village Fête is the highlight of the summer social calendar in Causses. The whole village of 556 pay 10 euros each to sit on long trestle tables, to eat a three-course meal with wine and watch a cabaret from a specially built stage. The Fête is for the village. The Fête is absolutely for the village and *only* for the village. The Fête is a bonding exercise of some proportion. Other Languedoc villages have their fête, and Causses has its Fête. And that is why it all kicked off.

As I sipped, I surveyed the scene. The honey-coloured stone of the medieval houses was exquisite. You could smell the thyme in the hot evening air languidly drifting down from the Montagnes Noires, which form the southern edge of the Massif Central. One or two bats had already squeezed from their daytime lodgings and were careening around the rooftops.

4

Swifts screeched in formation, down low then fast into the sky, round the tall stone buildings. In the Place du Marché the lowering sun touched the crimson pantiles, and all you could hear was the agreeable hubbub of voices.

Suddenly, out of the corner of my eye I detected a sharp movement accompanied by a shout. I turned just in time to see a small but stocky bloke about halfway down one of the trestles dive across it towards another burly son of the *terre*, who leaped back to watch the first fellow land stomach first onto a table that was designed for plates, pastries and bottles of wine, absolutely not fifteen stone of rural Frenchman. The table did what any table would do when treated in such a fashion: it collapsed with a huge crash, folding up metal legs and wooden top rather akin to those stuttering black-and-white films of early aeroplanes when they taxi and the wings fold up. Not without skill the lunged-at man was quick to seize the advantage and threw himself on his attacker with gusto and the thick end of a wine bottle. Now, you have to remember that the place is packed with a mixed attendance of young, old, males, females and children of every age from babes in buggies to toddlers and upwards. So, as in any self-respecting brawl, the usual happened: the old ladies and children and women screamed and scattered, and the blokes leaped up and headed for the fun. In an instant there was a boiling mass of bodies flailing like dervishes at anything that moved. Moments later, a few casualties began to retire to the sidelines, heads gashed, blood seeping. From the left an old lady in bombazine screamed. From the right a more energetic elderly woman wailing with frightened tears realized she was actually having rather more fun than she had had in years and, clasping her walking stick, made for the nearest combatant. But when a likely body ripe for bashing spun out from the mêlée, she thought better of the expedition, reverted to a touch of the vapours, and retired to a safe distance to be fanned and recover. Young fellows looking for glory piled in; men in their twenties looking for stature with their lady friends piled in; men in their thirties looking for diversion piled in; men in their forties looking to give anyone a damn good hiding for being younger and fitter than them piled in; and men in the fifties, sixties and seventies not so much piled in as clustered around the main action picking off stragglers with a well-planted thump. All was fair trade.

Just as the initial heat had passed and combatants were starting to back off and posture, onto the scene strode Monsieur le Maire. Ah, Monsieur le Maire. Like a portly Gary Cooper he strode through the parting crowd. In one fluid movement he stepped up, grabbed the first body he could see and planted a bone-shattering fist onto the top of his head. The receiver of the blow turned to take on his new foe but, seeing who it was, thought better and moved gingerly aside. At this point, a collective sixth sense amongst the brawlers set in, and everything suddenly stopped, leaving the man who had started it all bloody and unbowed isolated in the middle, panting, his fists clenched, face streaming with blood, and the expression of a cornered alley cat. He wasn't afraid of Monsieur le Maire. No sir. He stood his ground. Monsieur le Maire, seeing his work was done, indicated to two strapping citizens behind the outlaw to grab his arms. They pounced before he could see what was happening and was thoroughly clamped no matter how fiercely he struggled. Exhausted, he suddenly decided that he had better explain himself and began shouting, '*Je ne m'inquiète pas. Je ne m'inquiète pas. J'ai payé comme chacun!*'

Just then I noticed Monsieur le Butcher had arrived at my side. He whispered, 'He's from M-m-m-murviel. Trying to sit in on our Fête. M-m-m-murviel. They're all v-villains in M-m-murviel. Look at him: steal your m-mother. You can never trust anyone from M-m-murviel. The m-meat's bad and the b-bread's stale and when they deliver wood it never b-burns.'

The miscreant was frog-marched past us out towards the main road still shouting. Monsieur le Butcher shook his sweating, bald head and flicked his chin at the interloper, who by now was staggering into the main road demanding justice and howling that the men of Causses were women.

Around the square men congratulated each other on their bravery. Those that were blooded were now a fraternity, and aeons hence they will recount the brawl, and those who were there will strip their sleeves and show their scars. A year later, I was chatting to our plumber, and he mentioned that it was a shame we missed the excitement last year, when there was a monumental fight. 'Apparently,' he said gravely, 'there were many taken to hospital, and one man from another village was nearly killed.'

Later, as the feast commenced, we repaired to our roof terrace the other side of the tenth-century church. We sipped iced rosé, sweated and sang along to '*Mack le Couteau*' courtesy of a rather good local chanteuse belting it out from the stage over the rooftops in the Place du Marché. I tapped the wall-hung thermometer. It was 30 degrees. I lay back on the warm tiles and gently basted. To our right, bats played in the medieval church tower, darting into the bell space then out again. An owl's weird shape silently crossed the spotlights and disappeared into the darkness.

When Freya and Kaz had drifted to bed, George and I talked into the night as we gazed at the twinkling cosmos. We talked of that which we know little but which we felt we might want to know more. We talked of stars and space and time, of people and places, beer and girls.

2

A Short Tour of the Mediterranean

What about the French? – a teenage encounter – grumpy
old man – L'Isle-sur-la-Sorgue – a place to look

As a youth I had an irrational dislike of the French, born out
of little more than a school exchange visit to Normandy when
I was fourteen.

Fifty years ago, it was quite an expedition to get to any part
of the continent. The trip started with a trek from the Midlands
down to Plymouth, where we caught a ferry to Roscoff, then a
coach to Coutances, a small cathedral town, which had taken
quite a pasting during the war. On arrival we all lined up in
the school car park and were picked by families to stay with as
if we were evacuees. One of the last, I was eventually claimed
by a middle-aged mother, bundled into a car and ended up, I
think by mistake, in a house brim full of five girls ranging
from about my age to twenty or so. And all they wanted to
do was look after me. And they used *tu* right from the start
like the French teacher said they would not – or at least she
said only people in families used *tu*. I was *as-tu soif*'d?, *as-tu
faim*'d?, *es-tu fatigué*'d? from morning to night. It was a fan-
tasy. The next day, when I went into classes, I was dropped off
by the eighteen-year-old. I might just as well have turned up
with Debbie Harry.

The girls were great, but their father was a monumental
pain. I was frightened to death of him. All he wanted to do was

talk to me in French, and all I wanted to do was stare goggle-eyed at his elder daughters. These two activities were definitely not compatible. It was here I had my first taste of a certain type of Frenchman which coloured my view of the nationality for quite a while.

I bought the most god-awful pound-shop cruet set in the shape of a pumpkin as a present for my parents and the newly released, vastly expensive Led Zeppelin album *Houses of the Holy* with the French sleeve for myself. The girls thought this was absolutely the right priority. Their father, on the other hand, had a complete sense of humour failure. Apparently, he was not a Zeppelin fan.

We had been looking for houses on the interweb and whatnot for a while. One evening, I was browsing this new thing called Google Earth, looking at places we had been to on the French Mediterranean coast and reminiscing to myself. The great thing about Google Earth is you become superman, flying from one place to the next in great sweeps, or hovering over patches of places like some satellite. It's a weird thing is Google Earth.

500 miles: To my right are Monaco and Milan, and just around the corner in Italy are San Marco and Rome. To my left are Andorra and Barcelona, and in the centre of the knobbly old geographical club that is Spain is Madrid. In the sea to my right are Sardinia and Corsica.

I know nothing about Sardinia.

I know nothing about Corsica for that matter.

Looking round to the left, I see Ibiza, Mallorca and Minorca. I've been to one of these. I spent a holiday in Mallorca once. That was when it was called Majorca as in 'the water in Majorca, don't taste like what it oughter'. I remember we stayed on the unspoilt part of the island. 'Unspoilt' means the part of the island that is full of bitter locals who despise you because they don't live on the spoilt part of the island, where their cousins have cashed in. They desperately want this to become the spoilt part so they can strike it rich. You, on the other hand, want to stay in a villa with no electricity and no indoor plumbing. I had a splendid time there, as it happens, except for some local nicking all my camera gear out of the back of the hire car when I had wandered down to a deserted beach for ten minutes.

I went to Barcelona once as well. Stayed in the Condes de Barcelona Hotel no less. If you know where it is, then you'll remember it has a balustrade around the front of the building with the flagpole sticking out of it like a Franco town hall. It was here I stayed in about 1985 in an air-conditioned suite. My employer was paying for a couple of nights for work, so I took my newly acquired wife for a bit of a do. When the work was over, we had to trundle down the road to a 1930s monstrosity of a minus one star hotel, which stank of cats' piss and had those clattering concertina doors to the lifts. At night you could hear the wailing of the inmates. That's where I learned the value of money.

100 miles: North of Marseille up the A7 is Provence. I know Provence pretty well: Gordes, Gault, Ménerbes, Roussillon, Apt, Aix and Cavaillon – a run-of-the-mill market town off the motorway, good Atac, *bricolage* and *gare* and a very convenient *périphérique* gets you out of there faster.

To the north-west of Cavaillon is L'Isle-sur-la-Sorgue. This rather beautiful market town has sold itself to the devil. It might look like a medieval village along the banks of a rather wonderful river as clear as a mountain stream with fish darting through lush green weed. It's not. It's actually the River Styx, and anyone who looks remotely local is in fact there to row souls across to the other side, where there is a bric-a-brac market which goes on forever. On midsummer Sundays they have boat races upstream conveniently taking one's mind off the heady redolence of *poulet rôti*.

I imagine forty or so years ago, when a few hippies arrived in what was then this sleepy rural market town with a knapsack and a few beads and trinkets to peddle, the locals thought how quaint and passed by with their bundles of wood on their backs and their Common Market loans – in proper francs – tumbling from their pockets in crumpled notes. Then by and by, the Parisians discovered the place and wanted to take home a souvenir or two of their rural moment. So the locals started to burgle their grandmothers' houses for 1950s kitchen scales and their grandfathers' sheds for old drill bits and wooden hand planes and sold them at the side of the road with prices thought up for a laugh the night before over a few pastis, written on those old white-card price-tags.* Raphaël and Chloé thought this terribly quaint and bought everything. Back in Paris they told their chums in the tenth arrondissement just off Quai de Valmy what a bargain they'd snagged. It was such fun that they came down the next year and paid a fortune for a rusty old nail and a mixed bag of goat's cheese. Now, every Sunday, L'Isle-sur-la-Sorgue is like an open-air Conran shop with concessions to the White Company and Rockett St George.

We spent many years going on holiday to a wonderful place near there called Murs, staying with a delightful lady called Anne White. She's English from Sussex and has lived in Provence for fifty years and is nearly acclimatized and accepted. Nearly. She's got another twenty years to go before the local *flics*

---

* It's amazing where they get those old white price-tags, the ones with the white cotton and oblong card attached; every stall has them, and they all seem to have the same handwriting. I suspect there's an old lady somewhere in the backstreets of L'Isle-sur-la-Sorgue in a medieval lockup writing these tags in the blood of kidnapped septuagenarian hippies.

let her off when she speeds. One of her stepchildren even married a local girl and has two Murs-ish children. But that only makes it worse. After all, he nabbed one of the local girls when there aren't enough to go round in the first place.

Moving west brings you past Orange to the Pont du Gard. On our annual holidays to Murs we would go there regularly to swim and marvel at this national monument: an aqueduct built by the Romans and in perfect condition. It's a truly breathtaking construction. Spectacular. If the Romans were to return, they would be thrilled, as it looks pretty much as it did when it was built. But it's not quite what it seems. It was in a mighty mess until the middle of the nineteenth century, when Napoleon III decided that the Republic should rebuild it. And that's exactly what they did, using stone taken from all over. So what you see is, in large part, not the Roman Pont du Gard at all. It's a strange thing. To Western sensibilities if something falls down and is replaced by the same thing, it's a replica. In the East, not so. The Kiyomizu-dera (Clear Water Temple) near Kyoto has been built and rebuilt many times over since it was first constructed 1,200 years or so ago. Ask a guide if it is the original temple, and there is no discussion. Of course it is. It is the embodiment of its own history. Its meaning and identity are not defined by its physical presence. In the West we have much more of a problem with this idea. If my grandfather had an axe, my father replaced the blade, and I replaced the handle, is this still my grandfather's axe?

25 miles: It's at about 25 miles that everything begins to get a little specific. You can start to pick out the coast and the vineyards, villages, mountains and the towns like Montpellier. I swooped down to look at the valley of the Orb river. Béziers: a famous rugby club and a rather splendid medieval cathedral, bullfights in the summer.

'Kaz, what do you know about the Languedoc?'

'You really haven't been listening, have you?'

'The listing on what is new?'

'Languedoc. Languedoc. That's where I've been looking for the last six weeks. That's where we are going to look next month. That's where we have booked to see five houses which I told you about in great detail last night.'

'Blimey, that's spooky,' I said.

3

Un Grand Projet

'Ryanair Elbow' and other martial arts – a Frenchman called
Charles from Lewisham – Nylon pillow fury – buying a house –
losing a house – a promise to see the good stuff

It was the month of March 2004, at about ten o'clock in the morning. The main concourse of Stansted airport was busy, at its centre the magnificent duty-free arcade said to have been built in 1991 to celebrate the arrival of Queen Elizabeth II in those parts. Kaz and I were chasing up and down with the hurried gait of budget airline passengers who seem to have limited time to give to everything. As Gabriel Chevallier had it: 'There was such chaos in all that we were saying to each other that we spoke with no intervals, probably a hundred words for every twenty steps. Frequently a single word, or an exclamation, served for a whole sentence; but these exclamations conveyed shades of meaning that were full of significance, for we were old companions, united in the pursuit of common aims and in the laying of foundations of a cherished scheme.'

We had booked ourselves onto a Ryanair flight from Stansted to Montpellier. If you are middle-aged, middle-class and can borrow a few bob, then a place in France is as important as owning a four-by-four, shopping at Ocado, having a Facebook profile you never use and being able to name every shade of Farrow & Ball in the swatch. (For the record I know none of these things and want none of these things.)

It had taken only four months for me to get to this position.

Kaz had decided from the get-go that the Languedoc should be the first port of call, as it was cheaper than Provence and somewhere new we could 'discover'.

That's my big problem. I cannot relax. If I'm relaxing I feel like I'm wasting time and should be working. If I'm working I want to get the work done as quickly as possible so that I don't have to work anymore. Believe me, I want to be able to kick back, to take it easy, to watch the world go by. I look at the clock and every tick is a death sentence. I try the deep breathing bit. I try to tell myself it doesn't matter, that there is plenty of time, that people won't think I'm an arse if I leave replying to their email for an hour. Try the traffic jam test on yourself. If I'm sitting in a traffic jam, I know there is absolutely no point in getting wound up into a purple frenzy because the traffic is not moving. I say to myself, 'You cannot do anything about it, stay calm.' Then I scream at the guy in front who has not moved into the two-foot space left by the guy in front of him.

It's the grumpy old man thing, although I got grumpy long before I got old. I was grumpy at the age of five. My mother tells the story of my first day at school. There was this big chap called Charlie Hines whose parents ran the local removals firm in Lichfield. I can actually remember the scene – or at least I think I can. I was led into this big Victorian classroom, high roof in that open Arts and Crafts style. Inside, little desks and chairs were laid out, and lots of mums with their children were milling around starting to say goodbye to their little loves. I was presented with a jigsaw of a blue steam train – bet it was Mallard. This looked good to me, and when my mum kissed me goodbye I just got down to the task. Then I heard a howl that sounded like someone was being bludgeoned to death. I looked up, and there was Charlie, arms outstretched, pleading with his mum not to leave. It was a heart-rending scene. Their first parting, a moment of pure pathos, a moment that probably scarred his life. I on the other hand just wanted him to shut the hell up so I could get on with my jigsaw. Charlie and I became chums later. Big fella. Being a small fella, it was good to have a school chum who was a big fella.

It went from bad to worse in my teenage years, all that hanging around in kitchens at parties. It carried on to college – why the hell did those shallow gits with the bumfluff manage to get the girls and not me, a man of depth and character, and bumfluff.

Grumpiness is just part of being a bloke. Since I lived in Lichfield, I was obliged to get to know about Samuel Johnson, who was grumpy as a stoat from the day he found himself crawling around in the gutter in Bore Street, trying to find his way home because he couldn't find his spectacles. Come to think about it, I distrust anyone who isn't just a little bit grumpy. I went to an interview with Sydney Pollack, the film director, and Frank Gehry, the architect, a few years back. They were asked how they had met. Much giggling from the two old men. You tell it, says Gehry; no, you tell, says Pollack, who then says: 'Well, it was after we were introduced at a reception in New York and we found we had spent nearly an hour in the corner bitching about critics and how us geniuses are always given grief by people who know nothing, and it was a tough old life . . . we realized that we would become good friends because all great male friendships are based on being fed up with everything.'

So Kaz had decided that we needed a project, and here we were in the queue at Stansted. The rest of those in line seemed to know each other. They all looked pretty well dressed and shod and were bandying prices. Prices of their tickets. An elderly well-dressed gentleman in a white fedora and a rather fine lightweight summer suit and his partner, a little younger with a bouffant hairdo, were first to the pitch. Seven of your English pounds each, though they did have the foresight to book at least three months in advance. It's the trick, you see: timing. Timing is everything. Or so you'd think, but that is only one thing that counts in the game of 'Ryanair-ticket-price-trump'. A younger couple with a Porsche key ring and a buggy packed full of privileged child were next to the wicket. Ninety-five pence! Yep, ninety-five pence, plus the airport tax of course, but the airport tax is neither here nor there. Ninety-five pence each. Each way. Less than two quid each. Less than four quid, since the kiddy comes free. How about that, then? Blimey, I thought, pretty good. Then it started to get competitive.

'You will have to check in the bags, you know that that's got to cost,' said someone from behind me as the queue shuffled forward.

'You've got to include airport tax, otherwise *it's not fair*,' suggested a veteran.

'And you've got to decide if it's just for the parents. I have to pay for my teenager, and that's not fair.'

They started to laugh and joke in the sort of way that people who are not part of the banter find completely unfunny. It got even less funny when I looked down at my ticket: 210 bleeding quid. I really hadn't got the hang of this.

After half an hour we got to the check-in, were issued boarding passes (this was a few years ago) and trotted off through customs and passport and security and whatnot. It had taken an hour so far. The flight itself was the total of one hour and forty-five minutes. We waited another half an hour until the flight was up on the board and then made for the gate. Mistake. The lags were there already and looked like they had been there a good while. They were at the front of the queue almost by the door to the gate. They had spread out as if they were having a picnic at Glyndebourne. Around them a whole suburb had accumulated. About 150 people were in two rows surrounding a bullpen, patrolled by two Ryanair people. One of them tapped the microphone: 'Ladies and gentlemen, welcome to this Ryanair flight FR632 to Montpellier. We'd like to inform you that the Ministry of Defence has just announced that World War Three has been declared and that there are a series of nuclear missiles heading in the direction of Stansted airport. We regret that we have only twelve spaces left in the secure fallout shelter. If you would like to form an orderly line with number one to one hundred on the left and one hundred upwards on the side next to the window, we will commence selection of the lucky dozen.' Like that's going to happen. Everyone – except us ingénues – surged forward, and I was introduced to the art of the 'Ryanair Elbow'.

'Ryanair Elbow' is a move from the same martial art as 'Commuter Train Shoulder', 'Baby Buggy Ankle' and 'Huge Bloke Stare' – you know the one where a huge bloke squeezes in next to you on the train and just stares at you menacingly for the whole journey for no apparent reason. Ryanair Elbow is not a straight, common-or-garden elbow up and into a rival's chest or arm. It's somehow much, much more than that. First, it's done in the crowd not out in the open. The arm comes up to about 45 degrees, and then there's almost a half-circle twist and the elbow prods perhaps two inches and is withdrawn and back down to the side in a flash. The best way I can describe it is as the budget airline Bruce Lee One Inch Punch. By the time you feel the pain, the perpetrator could have been any one of twenty people packed in around you. By the time the pain has subsided the culprit has gone, is down the ramp, across the tarmac and into their seat. By then, about twenty other people will have passed you by. These people are in league. They have training sessions in isolated farmhouses.

By the time we reached the ticket collectors we had gone from around fiftieth to around 150th and, more dangerously, been marked out as fresh meat.

We had just about sat down in the plane when the doors slammed behind us with the engines whirring; the air hostesses doing the life-jacket aerobics; the captain cross-checking; the dumpy truck pushing us out towards the runway and the person next to me reading the first of her 3 for 2s from Waterstones. Having spent nearly two hours getting to this point, it was as if Ryanair could not bear to have us on their plane. Without so much as a brake pedal being prodded we were on the runway, down it and up into the air. When we had just got through the clouds, the sales patter started. They wanted us off that thing as smartly as they could, but before that they were going to fleece us like a flock of penned sheep.

'Tasty beverages'. When was the last time you were offered anything that was referred to as a 'tasty beverage'? The last time I heard that phrase was from the lips of Samuel L. Jackson before he plastered a couple of youths all over their apartment with a very large handgun. Then came the sandwiches, biscuits, scratch cards and an advert for their preferred car hire company. I wondered if I could talk to someone about double glazing or an extended warranty on my CD player. Bear in mind this is a flight that lasts 105 minutes, so believe me they pack it in. What astonishes me most is that there are people who actually do 'partake' of the opportunity to indulge in a 'tasty beverage' and buy scratch cards. The scratch cards are announced as a way of giving to charity. Apparently you can win a car and in the late 1980s someone won one on a flight to Berlin.

I managed to resist the temptation of blowing my life savings on this 'tremendous opportunity', and within a minute or two we were taking the steep descent to Montpellier. Truth be told, getting off and picking up the hire car was a breeze, and we were soon on the motorway down the coast to Béziers, about 60 kilometres away, and then into winding country lanes pressed by vineyards either side.

We had booked to stay at a hotel that had been recommended on the interweb: Château Saint-Martin des Champs, a *relais du silence* – quiet hotel – and delightful it was too. I love out-of-season hotels, like out-of-season coastal resorts – that deserted, lonely feeling. Had they poisoned the marauding mass of sparrows that made more racket than a fire truck on Fifth Avenue, it might even have been idyllic.

Next day, we were up bright and early. The sun was shining, the sky was blue, the air was warm, the leaves were appearing on the trees, the rest of my chums were at work, and I wasn't. We pootled down to the nearest village, called Saint-Geniès-de-Fontédit, where we had arranged to meet the estate agent at a café called the Pachamunu. We got ourselves a coffee and croissant and waited for our *immobilier* and guide to appear.

Half an hour later, at around ten, up rocked Charles. I mean 'up rocked' literally. A filthy, powder-blue Renault drew up opposite the café with music thumping out from it. The music was silenced when the engine was switched off, and he clambered out, sunglasses on his head, eyes bloodshot, jeans and a shirt, late twenties. He tottered across the road, acknowledging *ça vas?* to almost everyone. Even passing cars wound down their windows and hooted their horns and shouted, '*Ça va*, Charles?', '*Salut*, Charles.' He waved with a heavy hand and a hard-fought smile, spotted us and with a sigh slumped down into the third metal chair round our table. 'Hey,' he said wearily in perfect English with just a trace of an accent, 'you must be the Dolbys.' Without leaning forward he put out his hand. We leant forward and shook it. 'Charles,' he said. 'I'm from Freddy's, the estate agent. Had a bit of a night. A few friends round and a couple of my wife's mates came down from Paris. Then I was up with our baby daughter after they left so I've not had much sleep. Anyway, I've got, I think, five or six places for you to see. We'll use my car, but I've got to stop off at the office to pick up the details. It's just around the corner. Want more coffee before we go? Sure you do. It's on me. I'll be a minute. By the way, what part of London are you from? I lived in Lewisham with my mother until about ten years ago. Shithole. Right, coffee? Yer? OK, give me a minute.' Here was our first introduction to the legendary Charles.

Twenty minutes later, he was back without coffee. 'OK, then let's be off.'

'No coffee, then?' I suggested.

'No time. You're here to see houses. I'm here to show you houses. Let's go.' So off we went, through country lanes and vineyards, through mountain passes, through villages that were tumbling down, into courtyards and through woods and copses and along straight roads arched with wonderful mottled-trunked planes. Well, I think we went through these places. We were going so fast and Charles was talking so much, not looking at any point in the direction we were rapidly moving, that the only way I could convince myself I was going to get out of this alive was by gazing at the dashboard and pretending I was in a coma.

On the outskirts of almost every village were rows of brand-new orange bungalows each with a spiky yucca out front. As we slowed into the old part of the village, every other house seemed to be tumbling down. I asked what was happening, and according to Charles when someone died most houses weren't inherited by one person, they went to everyone, and it generally took an age to sort out the legal niceties, leaving the house to the elements sometimes for many years. In any case, the locals didn't want to live in old, draughty, cold stone houses – big upkeep, and heating them in the winter was awful – so they moved to *lotissements* (housing estates) on the outskirts: much warmer and cheaper all round. It was the second-home owners who were snapping up the old places when they came onto the market. Charles said the locals didn't seem to mind much. They got the cash, and the incomers were pretty keen on making sure the houses were done up properly.

We stopped at a hamlet, parked up and were shown to a house that was as ramshackle as you could get. The locale was lovely – how could it not be, everywhere was lovely – but the place was tucked away in the hollow of the village with the entrance up a stairway. We walked straight into the living room to be greeted by a lady of around sixty who was 5 foot tall, 5 foot wide and nearly bald. She advanced towards us from the kitchen, wiping her hands with gusto on her clean white apron, and with a huge smile and much nodding of the head greeted us. There didn't seem to be anyone else in, so Charles ushered us round: one bedroom, another bedroom, and a loft full of stuff, and a hole in one wall that 'could be made into a roof terrace'. I got the feeling this would be a long exercise. Charles didn't so much as try and sell, rather moved us on. 'Not for you, I can tell,' he said halfway round. 'Come on.' Off he marched, saying, as far as I could tell, to the lady that it wasn't suitable, and with a wave of his hand we were off to the next location.

This went on for much of the day. One house after another until my head was about to explode. I think it was aversion therapy. Get the expectations down so that when something even remotely suitable came up then we would go for it.

The day ended around four with a drink in the bar. Charles was upbeat. 'Now I know your taste, tomorrow we can get down to work.'

'Great', I said and thought of my favourite armchair at home with a packet of Hula Hoops and a bucket of wine and the last episode of the second series of *The West Wing* just about to start. I sighed.

That evening, we sat after dinner in the cool garden of the hotel and decided that the chances were low, and that it would be a good weekend break if nothing else. The night set in, and the owls hooted, and we repaired to bed. That's when I lost it.

Nylon pillowcases! Now, excuse me, but what is that all about? Nylon effing pillowcases. You might just as well make the sheets out of pastry. You know when you put your head down and it feels like your cheek is resting on Velcro? Then the heat sets in, like embrocation without the smell. I was not amused. Major grump set in. Pillow goes across floor. A paroxysm of profanity. Down to reception, who just don't understand what I'm saying, even though they speak perfectly good Estuary English. It appears that these are the standard pillowcases and that's that. Strop factor fifteen. Stomp back upstairs, where Kaz is now reaping a whirlwind of discontent. I end up wrapping a towel around the offending article – don't say you've never done it, because you have. The night was a grumpy one until the morning, when, dazed and tired, the next round commenced.

Charles had had a good night's sleep and was spruce and ready to go. The first house was true to his word the previous evening: much more like it. A large townhouse on the edge of a village but needing too much work. The place was cut up

into small annexes that had been built into larger rooms. If you had ten times the asking price to do it up, it would have made a rather wonderful place. There was a terrace with marvellous views across the plain to the mountains. But not for us. Our small charabanc moved on from place to place with Charles never losing his enthusiasm. Having been born and brought up in France, but having also lived in south London, he spoke perfect English and perfect French and for all I knew perfect everything as well. He seemed to be one of those enviably sorted people. He was at ease. He was good at music and had worked at U2's studios in Dublin and reckoned he had carved his initials in the back of a mixing console – I'm sure Bono will go hunting for it when he reads this. His wife was an actress who had worked much in Paris and starred in a couple of French films. They were having a time of it, as she was being offered all sorts of roles in England and Hollywood – even though she didn't speak much English. There was a chance that if a film came up he would have to follow her to America, which he plainly wasn't enamoured about but said would do if he had to.

We pulled into the village of Magalas, parked in the square next to a pizza place and walked up past the medieval church round the corner and into a dense labyrinth of small cobblestone streets – which I later learned are called *calades* – lined with lovely old stone houses. We came to the one we were to look at. Blue shutters and a traditional blue-doored *cave*. Looked promising. We went in and opened the shutters to reveal a small living area with stairs off the back of the room and an open-plan kitchen to the left. Small but not bad and just restored. Still looked promising. Upstairs to another bedroom overlooking the street and another overlooking the house to the back. A small bathroom, but again all well done with stone walls uncovered and white paint making it look holiday home-ish not French house-ish. Upstairs and onto a small but perfectly well-done terrace overlooking the pantiled roof of the houses opposite and off into the fields and up to the mountains beyond. Nicely done all round. This was more like it. Small was the word, but practical and nicely done was the action. We liked it. Charles was enthusiastic also. He liked it. Thought it was just the job for a holiday home. Nice location in a nice village with good restaurants and bars. In fact, we would go and have a beer now, since it was nearly lunchtime.

We walked though the village, past the medieval church, past the butcher's that also doubled as a restaurant in the evening, past the first of two or three bars and past a small row of shops. It looked great. We sat and had a beer. This was good. Charles wanted to talk price: 130,000 euros all in. Strangely bang on the price we had been thinking about. We talked some more. Went back and had a second look. It had got better since we had left an hour before. It seemed a little bigger, and the two bedrooms seemed perfect: one for us and a shared one for the children. OK, they would fight a little as they got older, but who knows? We went back to the bar at Saint-Geniès. OK, let's go for it, I suggested, and we nodded. Charles phoned the proprietor and had a chat: we had offered the asking price. Smiles and nods. Off the phone. OK, it's yours!

Hurrah!

We then had to sign a note, to be faxed to the proprietor, write a cheque for 5 per cent of the price, and there would be a seven-day cooling-off period, after which things would move along.

Wonderful. Congratulations. We were the owners of a house in France. As simple as that. No palaver. No messing about. No fanfare.

Hurrah again!

Charles bade us farewell – he really did: 'Farewell,' he said – and we decided that a trip to the coast half an hour away was the ticket. We phoned George and Freya. Guess what? They were excited and wanted to know all, but we would go back and take some photos and call them later. We took some photographs of the outside of the house and set off for what looked like the closest part of the coast at Marseillan Plage, about 30 kilometres away. We were welcomed by a beautiful blue sky and a wonderful sandy beach stretching for miles and miles towards Sête. We parked the car and walked along the sand with hardly another person in sight. The wind was warm, and the sea was perfect. How clever we were.

Suddenly, I could hear the ring of a mobile phone. Out of habit I stopped and checked my pockets. Sure enough, it was my Nokia 3310. Unusually, I had left it on. Shrugging, I answered it, wondering who it could be. Perhaps the children had called back, too excited to wait.

'*Bonjour*. Monsieur Dolby?'

'*Oui.*'

'This is Freddy. Charles works for me.'

'Oh yes, Freddy, of course, it's your *immobilier*.'

'Yes, look, we have a problem.'

'Oh?'

'Yes, there's no easy way to tell you this, but there's been a terrible mix-up. The house you bought. I'm afraid it was sold a couple of hours before you bought it. The property was put on the market by a father and daughter. Charles spoke to the father, who, without realizing, agreed to your offer, but his daughter had already agreed a sale a couple of hours before. I'm terribly sorry, Monsieur Dolby. This is highly irregular. I don't think it's happened before in ten years. I do hope we can make this up to you.'

'Oh dear,' was about all I could muster. Somehow, somehow, I wasn't really disappointed.

'I'll make sure we make it up to you, Monsieur Dolby. I'll make sure that you are at the top of our list for new properties, and we will find you something.'

I think he was expecting me to go ballistic, but all I said was these things happen and we had had a nice trip. He suggested I was being very understanding. For grumpy me, I suppose I was.

He put the phone down and I explained to Kaz what had happened.

After all the euphoria, here we were deflated but somehow not fussed. 'Perhaps it just wasn't for us' went unsaid. We walked the beach in silence.

1 Place de l'Eglise

*An email from Freddy – we agree not to get our
hopes up – free to those that can afford it, expensive to
those that can't – 1 Place de l'Eglise*

We returned home, and I returned to work thinking we had
hit the bar and lost the match. Over the next couple of weeks,
we told our story to anyone who would sit still long enough.
Nothing came over on email. I thought our estate agent chum
had just fobbed us off with that story so we would disappear
back to Blighty and, with us being so far away, we would forget
about it. And that's what was happening. We got back into the
rhythm, and the idea began to fade.

Then, one evening about three weeks later, we got a personal
email from the *immobilier* man himself, Freddy. He was very
gracious and apologized again for our trouble and said that he
had attached a couple of house details which he thought we
might find interesting. They had not yet gone on the market,
and if we were interested we should contact him by return,
as they would be out in a couple of days and they would be
snapped up. I could almost see his index finger tapping the
side of his nose.

I opened the attachments. Blimey I thought. I called Kaz.
We opened the second attachment. 'Bleedin 'ell'. Here indeed
was the special stuff. Expensive to those who ask, free to those
who don't. There they were: a couple of large stone farmhouses,
tumbledown but not derelict, in the perfect area with character

galore. And the price, my dear, the price. Still out of our range, and we really didn't want to take on a farmhouse with all the maintenance. But, blimey, this was more like it. We were in. We were behind the counter of the butcher's at Royston Vasey. I had to stay calm and think how we could make the best of this. Gratitude. That was it, gratitude. Then lots of 'perhapses' and 'maybes' and 'we would be so grateful' – always worth going back to gratitude.

So I emailed my new best friend and said how grateful we were to him for keeping us in mind and that I hope he didn't feel I was taking advantage, but we were rather looking for more of a village house with room for a terrace, and it could be a little bigger, yes bigger, but we didn't want to be too much trouble.

He replied by return. No trouble at all, just leave it with him.

Then we started to panic. This was just too good to be true. He was testing us. He was having a giggle with Charlie boy, who would be on the line to us laughing his socks off before the hour was out. Ha! We got you there, he would say.

But nothing of the sort happened. A week later, another email came, and Kaz opened it like it was a Fabergé egg. Clicked on the attachments, and up pops this village house for renovation. She nearly freaked. The description was perfect. It was in fact just perfect. The pictures were a little skew-whiff, but she figured they had been snapped for us. She emailed back. Looks great. What to do? By return again our man replied. He was a little more serious this time. This was a good one, and we had it from that day – Thursday – to the Sunday, then it would be on the market on the Monday. We had three days. Three days to get out there, look at it and buy it.

Moving quickly, we decided only one of us could go, so Kaz made an appointment with the estate agent for 3 p.m. on

Saturday, and I booked myself onto a BA flight to Montpellier from Gatwick with an all-in ticket with one night in a 'Crap Hotel' in Montpellier – there is a chain of 'Crap Hotels' all over the world – and duly pitched up on Saturday morning.

Pretty mad thing to do, send one half of a couple to look at a house, you'll agree.

I arrived, hired a car and progressed via the motorway to Pézenas through Béziers, past Murviel and on to the village, where I parked the car. Looking at the pictures, I wound my way through the narrow streets and eventually walked through the arch to the church and compared the picture with the view.

Bugger, I thought, as I stood in front of the house in the wonderful church square. It's not going to wash. Too small. Beautiful village, though, the mountains behind and the plain down to the sea in front. Ah well. I got back into the car and phoned Kaz. 'Not going to work, old thing. It's just not right. Look, I'll meet Charles this afternoon and go and have a look anyway since I'm here.'

I repaired to the next village, called Cessenon, and found a bar called the Helder, grabbed a *formule* lunch of steak and chips, accompanied by a rather nice glass of tangy local white wine – Picpoul it said on the menu, I nodded at the waiter in appreciation – then met Charles at Saint-Geniès, got in his car and went back up to the village. I didn't tell him I'd already been. Good move. When we arrived, Charles led me to the house next to the one I had looked at that morning.

OK, I'm an arse. I'd focused on the wrong bit of the photograph.

Charles produced a huge iron key, the sort Renfield might have used to open his master's cellar, and advanced upon a door straight from central casting. My heart began to race. After a minute of fiddling, the door swung inward. and a gust of cold musty air tumbled from the darkness into the sun. Charles wasn't impressed.

'This is not a good idea.'

I said nothing. We stepped in, climbed four or five stone steps and turned left into the first room. It was pitch-dark. We staggered towards a crack of light, a broken pane in the window and a broken slat in the shutters. We groped around as Charles muttered about being told an electricity meter should be around here somewhere. We eventually found a lever, which looked circa Frankenstein's Castle, and Charles decided it was worth a shot, so heaved down on it. A clunk rather than a click and then a flicker as a fluorescent strip light stuttered tentatively to life.

The fluorescent tube threw out the sort of light you see in Wood-fall films. The broken window had obviously been letting in the elements for some time, and a swift had found its way through, got trapped, died and been mummified. On the floor was a layer of grubby linoleum, on the walls cracked and fissured off-white distemper. In one corner a stone butler's sink, now cracked and useless. Above it a single tap connected via a visible pipe that ran down from the ceiling. To the left was a black marble fireplace, and next to it a large old stove, which had blackened the walls and floor. A flue the colour of old leather drove up through the ceiling and into the darkness. Charles tugged a shutter, and light flooded in. He crossed over to the other side and creaked and juddered open a window, then crashed a pair of rotting shutters back against the monumental stone walls. In front of us, the Gothic arch of the church entrance was no more than 30 feet away. I wandered over to the first door, opened it and walked into the tack room from *Tess of the D'Urbervilles*. Everywhere were signs of long lives: black saddles hanging from huge black nails in the cracked limed ceiling, old fishing rods, pots, plaits of hops and dried vine cuttings, ages and ages old. The floor was covered in jars of every size, all open and empty. I edged my way to the window and opened it. Warm air drifted through. Across the square a man stopped, startled. I turned and looked up. An old wasps' nest, brown and papery, hung precariously from the beams. The layers of the nest were crumbling, and a fine caramel parchment powder had settled on the stone floor, pitted and cracked from unnumbered footsteps over hundreds of years. Here was the casual accumulation of this and that, telling the story of lives as precisely as a Pharoah's tomb.

Charles joined me. 'This is a nightmare. Let's close up, I've a couple of places down the road we can see.'

'No, let's look around.'

He shrugged.

I wandered back into the main room. Opposite, there was a pair of doors. I walked over and opened them. In the shadows I could see red flocked wallpaper, a black marble fireplace, floor-to-ceiling windows on my left and on the floor dusty and scuffed burgundy and white Languedoc crossed tiles hundreds of years old. The coving and the ceiling rose were once ornate, but now layer upon layer of white distemper made them look as if they had been piped from an icing bag. Next door there was another room the same. I went out to the stairwell. The quarry tiles – *tommettes* – were so old they were crumbling, and the wooden batten on the front of each step was worn and worm-ridden. I pulled open a huge oak door to reveal stairs curling up, round, out of sight. I climbed gingerly past a fall of plaster and a window blocked up with an old fertilizer bag. I turned left to find another room the same as the one below, a mirror of the first floor but full of old furniture covered in a thick, black, gritty dust, the accretion of years. Out and to the left again. We opened the shutters. It was a bedroom completely frozen in time. 'This must have been the old lady's bedroom,' said Charles.

'Old lady?'

'Yer, belonged to an old lady who died ten years ago. It's the son and grandson who are selling: the Petits. Their family have owned the place for a couple of hundred years, I think. Still live in the village. Work a couple of vineyards. The old lady was in her nineties.'

In the middle of the room was a huge nineteenth-century mahogany bed, all carved balusters and barley twists; a more solid bed you simply could not find. It was fully made up with pillows and a faded coloured quilt, and as with everything else, covered with the layer of thick black grit. On the obsidian fireplace were knick-knacks and two photo frames with black-and-white photographs taken, from the look of the clothing, in the 1920s. A handsome man and pretty woman. She in a dark long dress and bonnet, he in a tight smart suit and hat. Another with a donkey cart, which would have looked just as at home in Sussex or Maine. On the walls were large framed pictures of Madame de France flag-waving. Next door was a dressing room full of clothes on the floor and on a rail in the middle of the room. I touched the hem of one, and it disintegrated in my hand. I tapped the top of another and it powdered to dust.

We moved on up the crumbling stairs past another window, and at the top I threaded my way into a *pigeonnier*. The floor was rotten, and the lime now yellow. Above me pantiles, two windows open to the elements and various small pigeon-sized holes for the birds to come and go. It had not been used for decades, but there was still that smell of dusty guano. Down the two or three steps to the main stairs again and then into the attic. Great beams held up the roof and six or seven small windows. The floor was covered with a thick mulch of powdery, sweet-smelling dry hay. Through a small doorway was another room, the roof tiles slanting down to a far wall pierced by double hay doors and a pulley to bring the fodder up from the street. The two rooms ran the whole length of the house, 20 metres from end to end.

'Would they have kept livestock up here?' I asked Charles.

'Dunno,' he said kicking at some hay. 'Do you want to see the *cave*?'

'*Cave*?'

'Cellar'.

'There's a cellar as well?'

'So I'm told.'

We wound our way back down and out of the front door, walked through the stone arch that connects the church square to the larger square called Place Jules Milhau and walked down to an ancient wooden door, the stone surround so weathered it looked like it had melted. We shoved and crunched it open and went inside. It took a moment for our eyes to become accustomed to the dark. Gently the glory of the *cave* came into view. A vaulted roof, stone slits, stone walls over a metre thick, two huge wine vats, stone troughs along the back of part of the *cave* looking like they had been chipped from a mountainside. Agog, I crept over to the troughs, still full of hay, and looked up. Above me was an open 'chimney' right to the attic.

'So they kept the hay in the roof to keep the place warm and to store it and then they just pushed it down this shoot straight into the troughs for the animals who lived in the *cave*?'

'*Grenier*.'

'Sorry?'

'*Grenier* – the attic is called a *grenier*.'

'Charles, this place is just amazing, brilliant, fabulous. It's just completely wonderful.'

'It's bloody derelict. It's your worst nightmare. Come on, let's go and see these couple of houses I've got up my sleeve, all renovated and lived in. You'll love it. Lock the door and forget it. This place has money pit written all over it.'

'How much do they want for it?'

'A hundred thousand euros.* There you go, that did it, didn't it? Back to your senses now, eh?'

'Would they take an offer?'

'What? Like they give you 100,000 euros to take it off their hands?'

'No, seriously.'

'Dunno. Look, you need a drink. Let's go to the bar, and I'll talk some sense into you.'

Two hours later we were back in the bar at Saint-Geniès. Charles had got the beers in and he was about as animated as I'd ever seen him: he had walked to the bar and back in less than ten minutes. He plonked the beers down. 'Well, as I say, I think you would be nuts,' he said. I was so excited I could hardly hold a thought in my head. I don't think I'd said anything for almost an hour. I took a drink – they only serve *pression* in those piddly little 250 ml glasses, so they go down pretty quick when you're used to pints.

'Look, there's a couple of other places I'll show you this afternoon. You would be nuts, you know?' I heard Charles speaking in the background somewhere. The French call it *coup de foudre*.

I finished my beer.

'So what do you think if I offered them eighty?'

* In those far-off days the exchange rate was 1.51.

'Leave me out of this. You want to have a midlife crisis then that's your issue.'

'Seriously. How much?'

'OK, seriously. They will want the asking price.'

'Why?'

'Because some nutcase will pay it.'

'Offer them eighty.'

'OK.'

He made a call.

'They said they want the asking price.'

Charles and I played pool most of the rest of the evening. I couldn't concentrate, so he beat me hands down. Had I had my mind on the subject I could have taken him, easy. I drove back to the Crap Hotel in Montpellier and called Kaz and went through the day's events.

'They definitely won't go for eighty, then?'

'Nope. Let's talk when I get home.'

I had dinner in a small place near the University, slept badly and got home the next evening tired beyond belief. We talked, and Kaz said I should do what I thought best. She hadn't seen it. It was up to me.

5

Yours . . . Kind Of

Ed Victor – villages – things you should know – things
you should do – bar etiquette – bread

I was rolling on a pair of Agent Provocateur stockings when
Ed Victor called.

'Trevor . . . ? Ed. I have news. Paul McGuinness and the
Boys would like you to publish their book. Congratulations.'
My stick of Ruby Woo slithered up my cheek in shock.

'Great news, Ed. You've caught me in my cerise fishnets and
pink high-heels.'*

A moment's silence as Mr Ed Victor, CBE, doyen of the literary scene in London and New York for forty years, über agent
to a glittering pantheon of musicians, writers, journalists, poli-
ticians, restaurateurs and actors – Mel Brooks, Andrew Marr,
John Banville, Nigella Lawson, Iris Murdoch, Freddy Forsyth,
Tina Brown, Alastair Campbell, Kathy Lette, Eric Clapton,
Keith Richards, Douglas Adams, Will Self, Erica Jong – the
man whose name was synonymous with the words 'dazzling'
and 'star-studded', the man with the ability to walk into a room
of publishers with just a name and an idea and walk out with

---

* For the record I was making up for a rehearsal of the Publishers' Panto-
mime, a huge charitable undertaking that used to take place every three years,
though the last one was in 2006. I was playing the Deputy Head Girl in a raucous Ronald Searle-endorsed St Trinian's pastiche, *Quid Quid Ipsum Vendit (or
Whatever Sells)*. I have to say, with all humility, I was simply gorgeous.

a five million dollar cheque, says: 'Stockings, I assume? I don't approve of tights.'

I had known Ed on and off for fifteen years up to that point. He the star that publishing revolved around, me a small tumbling asteroid in the wannabe belt. Ed Victor was smarter than me, more stylish, better connected, wealthier than me – by some millions – funnier than me, more articulate than me, taller than me – by some margin – slimmer and fitter than me, even though he was nearly twenty years my senior. But when I got to know him, I realized the thing about Ed was that none of this actually mattered. If he liked you he treated you the same: rock star, royalty and lowly publisher. He was kind and respectful of everyone. Polite, straightforward and truthful with everyone. Not just people who might do him good.

Once, when I left a job under a cloud (I'd been fired), my confidence was bust, and to put the tin lid on things I had had to have an operation. Ed heard and called.

'Trevor . . . ? Ed. I have booked a table at the Ivy Tuesday next week. Be there at one.'

I was low.

'Thanks, Ed, that's kind of you, but I've just had this op and I'm being told I need to rest.'

'Rest at the Ivy.'

I pitched up and was led hobbling to the banquettes at the back facing the entrance – all the better to see you all. Ed arrived, and we talked. Or, more precisely, he talked. He talked about work and about people. He told me stories about tenacity, getting back on the horse, about learning and battling on and the struggle between doing what you feel is right and fitting in. 'Mavericks have more fun,' he said. I liked that.

Late into the afternoon, we were still there, and he was smiling, and I was giggling, and he was allowing me to rib him a little. I kept saying he must get on, that I was taking up too much of his time. He wafted my protests aside. By four I said I would get the bill – 'It's the least I can do for your kindness'. He placed his hand on the table.

'Trevor . . . you will do no such thing. I will pay, but you must promise me one thing.' He eyeballed me. 'You will not become an agent. I need people to sell to.' It was his oft-used line to editors, but I was flattered and bolstered, as I was meant to be, and I left with almost a spring in my step. The one thing Ed could not do was heal a hernia operation.

The Monday after I got back that first time from seeing 1 Place de l'Eglise, I had a longstanding lunch date with Ed. We met, and I told him the story.

'Trevor . . . Can you afford it?' he asked.

'Well, not really, we've borrowed the money.'

'Will it go up in value even if you do nothing with it?'

'No. It will probably lose money whatever we do with it.'

'Do you love it?'

'Yes.'

'Then buy it. Life is too short. Phone them, and I shall buy lunch while you buy a house.' I've met few people who loved a deal more than Ed.

Just a few minutes and it was done. I put my phone down and announced it to Ed, triumphant that I had done it. He ordered champagne and he proposed a toast. 'Congratulations! Here's to your new adventure and my annual free week in the south of France for brokering the deal. *Santé!*'

I called Kaz, who was also delighted, and Ed and I tucked into I cannot remember what, as he told me stories of half a century before when he lived for a year in Loupian, which we realized was just a few kilometres away from my recently bought house. It was the late 1960s or early 1970s, and he and his new wife Carol had upped sticks for a few months to decide what to do with their lives. 'You'll be happy there,' he said. 'Loupian was a time in my life when the sun shone and money was worth nothing. We lived on cheap oysters from Bouzigues just across the fields, wine *en vrac*. If a battered Citroën appeared, the village turned out to admire. A couple of kilometres away [where now the main D613 road from Béziers to Montpellier slices though the vineyards and lorries and BMWs race along the coast], the main road was just a dust track with horses and carts.'

There's a black-and-white photo of Ed and his wife Carol from about this time. Ed bearded, huge hair, cheesecloth shirt, bell-bottoms. Carol by his side, smiling, standing in front of a brightly lit window, confident and happy.

A month or so later, Kaz and I flew to Montpellier, hired a car and hot-wheeled it over to the *notaire* in Autignac, a village nearby, to sign the deeds. The deeds done, we took the Renfield keys and excitedly drove over to Causses.

In 2004, the village was still much as it had been for 100 years. Place Jules Milhau had not been zhuzhed up with new tiling and drains. Place du Marché was still Place du Marché not Place de la Pompe Neuve. Dido was in residence in the bar, Marie-Claire lived next door. Many of the old medieval houses in the centre of the small *circulade* were crumbling – like ours still is, we like to keep up the old-world charm. La Maurine Cave was still in the old building off the Rue des Forges, not in its soon-to-be-constructed, architect-designed showroom on Victor Hugo – which lasted about five years before La Maurine owner Sébastian Collot sold it. There were a few English in the village, retired couples for the most part; I don't recall any holiday houses. But within about six months of buying 1 Place de l'Eglise, there seemed to be a frenzy of buyers particularly from Sweden who had discovered the village and the area thanks to our go-ahead *immobilier*, Freddy. He had put in some adverts in the local Malmö newspapers after he had had some inquiries from the area, and over the years the Swedes have become quite a community: Hans and Lotten opposite us, Bengt and Nette, Sandra and Aje among them. Every year, the Swedes from around the area hold a service at the Eglise Sainte-Marie du Pin in Vieussan up in the mountains. We were invited once, and there must have been seventy or eighty people. We were the only English people there. Quite the honour.

At that time, entry to the village top and bottom was just road. Now, thanks to the euro millions (not the Lotto but the grants that come from Brussels for useless infrastructure, which the locals look on much like the Lotto), we have St Tropez-like traffic islands and pine-treed picnic areas and a plush car park for people who are going on the 14.5k *randonnée* into the vineyards. There's a rumour that when it was all constructed, at the following New Year's knees-up (more of that later), the gathered were listening to the mayor proudly announcing its completion. There was much applause. He continued that there had, however, been a bit of an issue, and the little pull-off roads for the bus to pick up passengers were actually too small for the buses to get in and out of. Apparently the cheers were deafening.

It was difficult to tell what the locals thought of all us invaders. They had seen nothing like it. Some probably muttered 'Parisians' under their breath. In terms of the way the village was run nothing changed and still hasn't. As in villages the world over, those whose families have lived there for generations hold sway. Those who have just arrived need to understand their place. There is the wonderful story of Maurice the rooster on the Ile d'Oléron just north of Bordeaux whose owner was sued by a new holiday house owner for cock-a-doodle-dooing too loudly in the mornings. Maurice's owner, Madame Fesseau, who has lived on the island for thirty-five years, a retired waitress and now chanteuse, said, 'A rooster needs to express himself.' Christophe Sueur, the mayor of the village, was grave: 'We have French values, we have to defend them. One of these traditions is to have farm animals. If you come to Oléron, you have to accept what's here. This is the height of intolerance – you have to accept local traditions.' Maurice won the day and was of course *coq*-a-hoop. Then there's the story of the woman on holiday who stormed into the local mayor's office and told him to stop the bells ringing at night because it was waking her up. These tales are legion.*

In the mid-1970s my father and mother moved to a small village in Derbyshire. It was pretty much run by three farming families who owned most of the land thereabouts. The heads of the families had their own pewter tankards behind the bar at the local pub and decided things in front of roaring fires in back rooms. Half the village cemetery was taken up by their relatives going back 300 years. These families had sewn up the parish council for generations and granted each other planning permission for whatever they wanted and wherever they wanted it. If you have ever read Winston Graham's *Poldark* or watched the TV series, you'll get the picture. The place was run on the basis of my great-great-grandfather scratched your

---

* In January 2021, a 'sensory heritage law' was passed. Now if Maurice wakes you up on your *vacances*, tough. Likewise, birds singing in the trees, church bells ringing and the rich perfume of manure in a farmyard. I just bloody love the French.

great-great-grandfather's back, and that's the way it is. No great-great-grandfather back-scratching and you have no business in front of this roaring fire, my friend. After a parish council meeting, suddenly planning permission would be given for a 'farm building' in the middle of a field, or on the top of a hill where the view across the valley just happened to be wonderful for the 'cows'. Except the farm building that appeared for a brother or retiring father looked rather like a bungalow with a double garage, garden, vegetable plot and swimming pool.

When my parents arrived, the parish hall was falling down, full of dry rot, roofed in pressed asbestos. It was never used and was running to derelict. By and by, a couple of people got together and decided to see if they could get it repaired, and my father took on the role of treasurer – I think it was treasurer, in any event he was heavily involved in raising money and renovation. It took three or four years and was a big thing for a small community. It was a great success. Forty or so years later it is still the heart and hub of the village. The Parish Hall Committee was thanked, and all moved on. Not long after, my father was asked by some of the newbies (i.e. those who had only been in the village a few decades) if he would be happy to be put up for the parish council. He was not bothered either way but said OK. There was a meeting, his name was mentioned, and from 'the families' there came utter derision. A newcomer? On the parish council? Laughable. Come back in 100 years when you've earned the right. Things were about to change. Not long later, district councils started to take a closer look at the workings of parish councils all over the country.

Here are a few pointers on how to behave when you first arrive in a French village. First, get out and about; say *bonjour* in a jolly fashion to anything that moves. But don't be tempted to stop if your smile is returned and you are bonjoured *Messieurs-dames*. *Bonjour* is quite sufficient at this stage. Only say more if you are invited to by the bonjourer. Then answer questions only and move on – but don't seem to hurry – with another smile and an *allez*, or *bonne journée* or *allons-y* if you are with a companion or dog. Do not be tempted to ask questions unless it is advice on 'the best place to get . . . '. No 'Where do you live?' or 'Where's the best restaurant?' For the moment, that's none of your business. If your French is as bad as mine, then it's the effort that counts, but don't push it. Dogs are great to oil the social wheels, but remember in rural France dogs are not part of the family, they are employees. Be interested but don't go all gooey over them. If you do, either they or their owner will bite you.

We were talking to one of our longtime neighbours a year or so back. We bump into him rather than rendezvous – that's how things are done. René speaks pretty good English, but quite rightly you don't speak English in a French village, particularly to someone who lives there. René's son lives in Texas, and his wife, Brigitte Thiltges, runs a terrific little atelier, 'Les Arts du Jardin', making place-settings, candle-holders, table centres and whatnot out of local found materials. We got chatting about someone not far away who had moved in and was doing major work to their house and yet had not knocked on René's door with a bottle of good local wine to tell him and apologize for any inconvenience. It appeared they had just pitched up without a by-your-leave and cracked on. They hadn't even asked for advice. Very important to ask for advice in these situations, even if you don't need it. I said that we were probably guilty of doing that. '*Non!*' he said. You made an effort. He remembered first meeting us, when we knew nothing, and he was impressed that we had been friendly, even

46

though we could hardly say anything other than *bonjour* and *oui*. That was over a decade before. Always remember, villagers always remember.

A few years back we went on a hike with the local walking group organized by Michel Bonnafous. We were recommended by John Andrews, the first full-time *Britannique* in the village and by then, some years later, an honorary Caussanais. A recommendation was not strictly required but it was polite. 'A friend of yours is our friend, John' was always the reply. There were a number of new faces who, it transpired, had recently returned to the village after retiring from Airbus in Toulouse. One fellow with all the right walking gear had been an engineer for thirty years, travelling the world. He was proud to have worked for Airbus and proud to have now returned to his roots. As we talked, I was interrogated. In French. My brain nearly burst trying to find the words to answer his questions, circling my slim vocabulary to locate anything to give the gist. When we got back to the village, I managed to tell him about our *cave*, which is pretty much the oldest place in the village outside of the church. He knew of it but had not seen it and was keen, so I opened it up and shone a torch in, trying to find a way to describe the barrel roof. His eyes lit up, and he got out his own torch attached to his walking staff, then proceeded to give me a technical talk in perfect English about medieval Mediterranean architecture.

The next thing is to visit the bar. You may not like the bar. You may not like bars *per se*. But you need to visit the bar. Here again, follow the etiquette (etiquette: from the French word for 'label', appropriated by the English from the cards printed and handed out to prescribe how to behave at the French court). Be as friendly as possible with the owner and the barman. My chum at Le Helder at Cessenon has been there all the time we have been here. I've watched him go from bouncing youth to bouncing middle age. We get along because I encourage him to correct my French. I call him Professor. And he likes to practise his English. I teach him swear words. Perfect exchange.

Be aware of the locals in the bar. They will be in the bar at their own regular seat. They have their own regular times to visit and they will be drinking Pastis 51, Ricard or Pernod. I know that's a cliché, but it's true. The younger ones perhaps *une bière pression* – draught lager – ordered as *une demie*. Do say *bonjour* and smile. They will probably ignore you. But that's OK. Keep smiling. Don't attempt to get a round in as a way of buying your popularity. They will willingly take your offer, but you'll be known as flash and pushy. Say *bonjour*. Order and stay quiet. No loud talk. Nod if anyone looks in your direction. If you happen to sit next to someone at the bar and they talk to you, all good. Apologize if your French is not up to much and say that you are learning and you would be grateful if they would correct you. They like that. Power transfer. The local dialect is always good to pick up. In Languedoc the accent is pretty broad. Think Geordie or Brummie. They tend to emphasize the end of words with 'uh' – for example, *baguette-uh*, *bière-uh* – and they don't say *oui*, they say *weh*. Just a couple of nuances like that can make all the difference.

Seek out the bakery or *dépôt de pain*. Every village and town has at least one *boulangerie*. If the village is too remote or simply too small to support a bakery, then they must have somewhere they can import dough to cook on site or fresh bread from nearby, daily. No matter how remote. It's the law. Bread is a serious business in France. The French Revolution was all about grain, the lack of it, to make bread. In the 1780s, 80 per cent of a rural French person's diet was bread. The principal responsibility of the monarchy, apart from spending money and shagging, was to make sure there was a good supply of grain to the people. In that capacity the King was known as *le premier boulanger du royaume*, First Baker of the Kingdom. Before the Revolution, as things got worse and, in an attempt to ingratiate himself with the people, it was put about that the King ate *maslin* bread, which is what the peasants ate, instead of the posh *manchet* bread. To encourage the bourgeoisie to rise up, the revolutionaries proposed that they should do everything they could to ensure the lack of bread. They actually impeded the delivery of grain and blamed it on the King. It worked rather well.

As recently as 1993, in a law called 'Le Decret de Pain', the ingredients of each type of bread sold is defined in minute detail. Bread, and wine of course, is hugely symbolic: the more you know about the different types, the textures and the recipes, the more you will both understand the French and be respected down the bar.

6

Road Trip

A van full of domestics – demolishing a roof – the benefits of air conditioning – dogs and other nationalities – removal men – bullfight

It had taken George and me ten hours to get from Calais to Pouilly-Fuissé in a furniture-packed white High Top Ford Transit hired from Hertz on the Old Kent Road. There was no air conditioning, and the temperature was unbearable. It was mid-July, and I was pulsating with heat. I was within a smidgeon of self-combusting from the inside. My temples were the colour of boiled langoustine. My nose was like the end of a tropical leaf in a rainstorm. George was no better. He had stripped down to his boxers and was beginning to bruise. We dared not speak to each other as the movement of our jaws would up our temperature by a tenth of a tenth of a degree. To make matters worse, we had been looking for the hotel we had booked ourselves into for about an hour since leaving the A6 near Mâcon. Suddenly George spotted a sign with the hotel's name on it. It was like we had spotted a red neon arrow in the desert signposting Jesus and cold beer. I floored the accelerator, and we crashed down the lane. There it was in front of us in the twilight: a pool, a restaurant, air conditioning. My eyes glazed over, and I just went for it, spun the van into the drive down the ramp past the packed terrace full of diners and round into the car park. Well, that was the plan. You see, in all this excitement I had forgotten that I was driving a van over 3 metres high and that unless you give overhanging pantile roofs sufficient berth they tend to gouge deep holes in metal when they collide at 15 kilometres per hour. And that's exactly what happened. An almighty crash, and I slammed on the brakes, nearly bringing a ton of furniture, books, beds, bed linen, towels, pillows, tables, chairs and all manner of household goodies into the cab with us, out onto the bonnet and into the road in front. I looked at George. 'Bugger.'

George had an insouciance way beyond his then sixteen years. His reply fitted the moment. 'Bugger indeed,' he said in a pretty fair imitation of Stephen Fry as Jeeves. There was a pause. 'Sod it,' I said, 'let's go get a drink.' With this, I moved off slowly, the grinding noise getting worse and worse until suddenly there was a clatter and we were free. 'Pretend nothing happened,' I suggested as we drove 10 metres into the car park and came to a halt. I switched off the engine. 'Sounds good to me,' agreed George, 'but how do you suggest we persuade the forty people fifty feet away on the terrace eating their foie gras and frogs' legs that nothing happened?'

'Caution to the wind,' I said firmly like I knew what I was doing. He shrugged.

I grabbed our overnight bag, and we strolled out of the car park without looking round. I couldn't face finding out the damage to the van. I figured whatever happened I was in for the excess, so it was all pretty academic as to whether there was any roof left or a scratch. As we walked up, I swear the majority of punters had not moved from the moment we had appeared and nearly demolished their hotel. Indeed, I swear a few had frozen with a fork full of nosh halfway to their mouths.

We strolled up and past them to the reception. To emphasize the ruse, I decided to make friendly: '*Bonsoir, messieurs-dames,*' and nodded at everyone in as jolly a fashion as I could muster.

Their eyes followed me round with bemused nods. I had the full house: Englishman, cannot drive, memory loss. I dinged the bell at reception and waited for attendance, smiling at anyone who cast a glance. It was then I noticed that about four pantiles from the roof we had hit had found their way to the roadway, where they lay arse over tip. To boot, a small lamp, still lit, swung on its wire back and forth, back and forth. It reminded me of John the Savage hanging from the beam.

'Er, I think we may have left too much evidence to get away with this,' whispered George.

'It's getting dark. They won't notice, and the punters outside won't grass us up. They're French – they hate authority.'

'Yep, and that's why they will. We, lest you forget, are *le rosbif*.'

From a little cupboard in the back strode a large middle-aged woman dressed in gingham and with a bosom the size of an IKEA self-assembly sideboard. When we told her we were the Dolbys she was quite beside herself. She had given us up for lost and had almost let out our booked room. Weren't we lucky she had given us ten minutes more? '*Très chanceux*,' I suggested. I noticed she had a glass of rosé in her hand, which she placed next to the registration book. The glass was wet with misty moisture where the cold wine hit the warm air. I turned into John Mills transfixed by his glass of Carlsberg in the final scene of *Ice Cold in Alex*. The world faded into nothing, and all I could see was this glass of rosé. I crash-zoomed until it filled every corner of my vision. My hand started to move towards it when suddenly I felt a jab in the ribs. It was George. The woman behind the counter was saying something. I snapped out of it. Bugger, she's noticed the pantiles. But no, she was giving me the key to our room. Bingo, I thought, and we were off like whippets before she changed her mind.

George and I had been planning this road trip ever since

we had bought the house two years earlier. It was our boys' outing. An adventure before he was seventeen and old enough to start treating me with contempt. We had been accumulating bits and pieces for the house for all this time, and the plan had always been to transport them down in a van of some proportion, unload and then perhaps do the same once every couple of years thereafter. OK, I hear what you are saying. Why don't you buy stuff down there? Because, well, OK . . . I had hoped not to get into this. I admit it: eBay. Yes, yes, I've tried therapy. Yes, I've tried not switching on the computer. I've tried forgetting my password. I've deleted my credit card and I've danced with the devil in the pale moonlight, but nothing, nothing, has managed to wean me off eBay. It's methamphetamine for the middle classes. The crap I've bought. I once bought a plastic chandelier because it was 'exactly what we had been looking for and it was cheap and the other bloke who was bidding was just a little too cocky and I was buggered if I would lose to a two-bit chiseller like him . . . her . . . whoever'. Then there was the broken Christopher Dresser plate – I know I should have looked at the small print, but the auction was about to end, and I wanted it, so there. I've bought paintings that, on receipt, are always about half the size I expect them to be. I have this theory. You know these virtual reality websites, the ones where you can buy land, build houses and whatnot? There's even concerts in virtual concert halls. There will soon be logging onto a virtual computer in your virtual world and going in and buying virtual stuff on a virtual eBay. It's like mirrors reflected in mirrors. Call me old-fashioned, but I'd sooner get ripped off by a bloke I can see and punch.

Back in our room at the now part-pantile-less hotel, having wrapped ourselves around an air-conditioning unit and had two cold showers each, we plucked up enough courage to venture out. The only place to eat was on the terrace in among the witnesses. It was around nine, and most people seemed to have left, but a few were still there, trying to catch the little breeze that now fluttered through the trees in the humid evening air. No one now seemed to be interested in us, which was a relief, and we plonked ourselves down and ordered. It was then we got a lesson in the French and their dogs.

I like dogs. My mum and dad always had dogs. Three. All called Bob. That's one after the other. It would be silly to have three dogs called Bob all at the same time. I've always wanted a dog, but, living in London as I do with a garden the size of a squash court, I always thought it just not practical. We went down the 'Labradoodle' route once – they are not too big, they don't shed their fur and they don't smell, apparently. We sent an email to a breeder. We got a note back along the lines of:

Dear Sir,

Who in the name of Barbara Woodhouse do you think you are, emailing me out of the blue? Do you really think you are fit to even breathe in the direction of my divine animals? Let me spell this out. First, you live in London, where everyone is sex-crazed and on drugs; second, you've never even owned a dog before, so it's quite inconceivable that you know which end to wipe and which end to feed; third, you are male, which means you are inept, naive, and, in evolutionary terms, the dog should be looking after you. Get back in touch when you have moved out of London to Tunbridge Wells, become considerably richer and had a sex change.

Best wishes

After that, we gave up, and it took another six or seven years before we got a black Cocker Spaniel called Lola. As a footnote, George and I wanted a cat, but that got vetoed every time. According to Kaz, they are in league with Beelzebub.

We were just settling down to order, when I noticed a rather large German Shepherd sitting comfortably and quietly at the foot of the people at the next table. He had a beady eye on me. Its owners noticed I'd noticed and just smiled. Ah well, I thought, and carried on reading the menu. It was the usualish French country restaurant fare of coquille Saint-Jacques, sautéed frogs' legs, coq au vin, steak frites. George chose steak haché, and I some sort of white fish and a *demi* of rosé. The first glass was nectar, the second glass double nectar, and the third just made the world a better, better place. I sighed and leaned back in my chair. George was supping Coke and water hand over fist. The evening was warm and agreeable. We had forgiven the management for making the pool out of bounds after dark, and on cue a rustling zephyr moved the air.

Just then, a small, white, fluffy animal that is only just the same species as the German Shepherd arrived with its Belgian owners. I could tell they were Belgian by the way they carried their own food in a bag swinging by their side. It was at this moment that the dog under the table next to us sensed his genetic chum, and all hell broke loose. Now, that's quite normal. Same thing would have happened in Manhattan or Montrose or Macclesfield. What was interesting was the reaction of their owners. They couldn't have been anything other than French or Belgian. The French owner of the German Shepherd watched as their animal careened towards the Belgian powder puff. It was going to kill it in the most savage fashion, no doubt about it. It was going to spread blood and guts to the far corners of the restaurant, pool and partly pantiled barn. They would probably be picking Belgian dog brains off our Hertz rental High Top for decades. The owners, however, were completely oblivious to this. They smiled beatifically and tucked into their sweetmeats. As the tables tumbled, it might have had as much to do with them as the fall of the Third Dynasty in China. The Belgians, on the other hand, had slow motion syndrome. You know, the one that kicks in in a car crash. They saw the future, and it was without their pooch. They grabbed it from the ground and hugged it to their combined bosom. It was, of course, useless – the Shepherd just kept on coming, and its owners kept on noshing, and it all seemed just too, too inevitable. Until out of the corner of my eye I spied a third combatant. This was becoming like a bad day in doggy Baghdad. It was obviously the hotel owner's dog. How did I know it was the hotel owner's dog? The hotel owner was on the other end of it. How did I know that it was the hotel owner? A grinning photo in reception with *propriétaire* written underneath. It was then that I noticed what he had in the other hand: a selection of pieces from the pantiled roof which just an hour before had been on his tidily tiled barn. Now, with that in mind you can imagine what mood *monsieur* was in. His mongrel was dancing at his feet, and suddenly in races German Shepherd, hotel owner and dog go *cul* over *sein*, and like magic the pantile evidence spins up into the air and off into undergrowth just as our main course arrives. Job done, I thought, as I brought the first rather tasty mouthful to my ravenous face. George, too, noticed the evidence disappearing into the ether and we toasted our good luck. Chin, chin, I suggested with a sweep of my glass, like Bertie with a glass of Aunt Agatha's best port.

Next morning, we were off early. We were determined to get some miles under our wheels before the heat set in. Six hours later, we were weaving our way through Béziers, not quite yet nuclear on the heat scale but on the way. It was then we pulled up at the lights off the motorway, and the windscreen washers descended.

In the 2000s, there were windscreen washer gangs in the UK but not like the ones in the south of France. These guys were the SAS of windscreen washers. These guys should have been running European nations – and probably were. First, they spotted our foreign number plate; then they descended with grins and jolly dancing moves with the squeegee held aloft, and no matter how much I gesticulated that I didn't want my windscreen washed, they did so anyway, ending with a squeegee heart. So at that point, I thought, why not give them a euro or two, it's the least we can do. But now we were getting a little flustered, watching for the lights to change. We passed them a euro through the gap in the window. As the euro went from fingers to fingers, there was a clatter of coin against glass. Bugger, I thought, it's been dropped down the side of the seat. I reached for another euro and the same thing happened. Then, just as I was going for going for a third and the cars behind were starting to get agitated, I grew ears and a tail. Quite simply you think you've dropped the coin, but in fact the squeegee man has palmed it and in his other hand he has another coin which he clatters on the outside of the same window. *Et voilà!* Good old-fashioned sleight of hand.

Back on the road we arrived at Causses at about two in the afternoon. It was now kicking 40 degrees, and we were glugging water like marathon runners. Leaving the van in Place du Marché, we walked round to the Place Jules Milhau and turned right under the arch into Place de l'Eglise. I clanked open the door, searched around in the cool dark for the power switch, clicked it down, and the lights came on. It was far from habitable. We had been led to believe the painters would have finished. They hadn't. It wasn't a complete mess, but they were still in, and there was stuff everywhere. Not a problem, we thought, we just unload, pile everything in one room and we crash out on the roof for the night. George and I made a deal with each other. We'd unload first then we'd treat ourselves to a swim in the river to cool off.

My first job was to get the van into Place Jules Milhau. There was about 1 centimetre of space each side, and it took fifteen minutes for me to get through, scraping one side in the process – I figured that I was already in for the 800 quid excess so I thought we might go stock car racing on the way home.

Opening the back of the van was the start. There must have been around a ton of stuff in there held in by a mammoth solid beech table donated by one of our chums. It had taken four people to get it in in the first place, and now here we were, two of us to get it out of the van through the archway up a flight of stone steps into the winding stairwell through the living room and into the dining room. To keep the whole thing stable we had taken some wood and battened the table top in with a few nails. These were the first things off and then we had to lower it out as gently as possible. There was no one around to help. It was us against the table. We got some of the pillows still in their packaging and made a pad onto which we could drop it. I'd watched draymen do this often enough with barrels of beer. All was set.

I don't know if you've ever seen Eric Sykes' genius short film *The Plank*, made in 1967. It's a movie with no dialogue about the chaos that's caused by two workmen as they try and get a plank of wood from one place to another. If you have, you get the picture. We managed to drop the table top – which must weigh 200 kilos – onto the pillows. Then we decided

after much head-shaking that we had best try and 'walk it' through to the door in the Place de l'Eglise. Old blankets were placed under the corner, and I moved it forwards, tipping the opposite corner up and onto another blanket. Genius. We got through under the stone arch, and all was going swimmingly, so much so that we reckoned we had got it sussed. We battled on inch by inch up the steps into the living room and the dining room. We were exhausted when we laid it down on the floor. I was about as soaked with sweat as it's possible to be. Had I thrown a bucket of water over myself I could not have been more wet. George was the same. I staggered out into the heat and picked up a hot two-litre bottle of water we had stashed, and we sat next to the wall in the shade and glugged it down.

'Shit,' I said after a while, 'it's purgatory.'

'Let's just get it done,' said George.

We hefted ourselves to our feet and with determination went for it. Twenty boxes of books were shifted, each around 20 kilos apiece. Two benches, boxes of kitchen stuff, four mattresses and the beds – one we had had made in iron especially from a foundry in Deptford. Every fifteen minutes, we stopped for water. I treated it like being on a chain gang. Doggedly do it. Get it done. When the last piece was unloaded, it was around four in the afternoon. I couldn't have been more exhausted if I had been digging trenches in the Sahara. We tanked up on more water then made off at quite a lick to Roquebrun for our well-earned swim.

Turning right on the D19 past the Mairie on the right, then over the hill, bursting into the mountains. More natural beauty and drama you could not find. Montpeyroux is the first rise behind the village, the first crinkle that forms the mountains of the Montagne Noire folding higher and higher into the Auvergne. We rattled down the hill and into the Haute Languedoc National Park.

The water at Roquebrun was like an unexpected day return to heaven: warm, but cold enough to cool. We lay in the current and watched the sparkling rush go from silver to gold as the day turned in. Cars left the bank side, and still we bathed, two hours if it was a minute. Eventually, as we wrinkled and the evening breeze whispered through the willows, we made our way to the Excalibur Café at Magalas for pizza.

It was still just light when we arrived, and the town was packed. We parked on the outskirts and wandered up the hill past the chateau, wondering why it was so crowded. At the pizzeria we just managed to get a last table, but outside – all the canny folk had already got tables in the air-conditioned interior. We sat and sighed, realizing only then that there was a commotion at the bottom of the hill. We ordered then pottered off to see what was happening.

In the car park was our first local bullfight. A rather small bull stood in the middle of a miniature bullring with 3-metre-high metal fencing. Young bucks wearing not very convincing *traje de luces* and *montera* ran from one side of the rickety arena to the other, trying to grab one of the ribbons tied loosely to the bull's horns as they passed. Every time one connected, the crowd roared, and the bull perked up like a commanded gundog. As the boys got more daring they slapped his horns and he flashed at them with a toss of his head. The closer the runner got, the bigger the cheer. As they passed at full speed they would crash into the arena side, leap one foot onto a first wooden rail a metre high around the side, then onto the next behind that two metres high and then slam into a platform next to the fence. If a ribbon was bagged, the place went nuts. Now and again a footing would slip, and the runner would tumble to the ground behind one or other of the rails, and his companions would charge onto the ring to distract the bull as others would scoop him up dazed and dusty. Ten seconds would pass as the crowd hushed, then he would rise, shaking his head, hand held high, smiling. A cheer would erupt, and he would hobble a little for effect then leap like a gazelle up onto the rail he had missed and wave some more.

We were lucky and had caught the finale. The parade of the daring youths wound up the show as the bull was ushered meekly into a trailer. As the sun finally went down, we walked back up to the restaurant, the cheers still ringing and echoing around the houses.

Around ten, George and I arrived back at the house. We were so exhausted we each just gathered a sheet and a mattress and pitched ourselves on the terrace, where there was a hint of a breeze. Inside, it was sweltering. In the half-light I watched George's eyelids wilt, his face relax. Tired and happy, he gently fell asleep. A memory which soothes me still.

7

Speak as You Find

François – a bathroom – a kitchen – the men from
Marseille – the importance of lunch – long memories

You will need your builder. Just like you will need 'your' baker, 'your' butcher, 'your' bar. You'll need your builder, and he will need to be local. Even thinking about taking on someone from outside a 25-kilometre radius and you're finished. You may be tempted to bring in the lads from Warsaw. Don't. And you'll think about getting a couple of estimates, *devis*. That's fine, but they all know one another and they'll talk. If it's a big thing and many trades are required, you'll have to find and hire everyone separately. It's not so rare now that a whole job will be done by one builder from the bricks to the plumbing, electric and plastering and painting. But fifteen years ago, it was not the norm. Above all, take your time. These things are not to be rushed. Once started, your job may have to mesh with other jobs, an absence of three or four days, or sometimes a month or two without explanation should be expected. And then there are lunches.

We were introduced to François by our Swedish neighbours Hans and Lotten. We wanted our ancient copper bath tub installed (see chapter 12, 'Tale of a Tub' for full disclosure) and the bathroom doing – there was no bathroom in the house at all when we bought it, just a stone sink, and that was cracked perfectly in two with a single tap above it and a bucket beneath the crack. François is an exacting fellow. He speaks English but only so there is no ambiguity. He likes to joke in the trademarked French way. Trademarked French humour goes as follows:

'Here's the bath and here's where I would like it installed.'

'But that's easy. Why do you want me to charge you money to install it? You could do that.'

'I'm not a plumber and I haven't the slightest idea how to install it.'

'But it's easy. Even you could do it. For half the cost of me installing it. I'll train you how.'

'How about I get someone else to do it?' He now backs away hands in front of himself as if fending me off.

'Hey! Just a joke. I'll do it. Of course I'll do it. It's a fine bath.' Turning to Kaz conspiratorially: 'He's very touchy, your husband.'

François came and installed the bath. Every time I came in to see how he was doing, he would stop and ask me to come in and look at his handiwork, insisting I should admire it.

'Can you help me for a moment?'

'Of course.'

'Hold this for me and hand it to me when I ask for it.'

He hands me an adjustable wrench. I stand with it as he disappears behind the bath with some sealant.

I stand there for a couple of minutes. 'Do you need this yet?' Silence for another couple of minutes. Then he appears, stifling laughter.

'You English, eh?'

I put down the wrench, laugh a fake belly laugh and walk off.

François came back and did the kitchen a couple of years later. We had some ideas sketched out for him. He looked them over one evening after we had opened a bottle of Picpoul. He concentrated hard for about five minutes and then took out a pencil.

'Are you sure this is how you want it?'

'Well, they are just ideas. What would you suggest?'

'What are kitchens like in London?'

'Well, err, kitchen-like . . . kitchens: cooker, fridge, work-tops, shelves, that sort of thing.'

He looks at me. 'Do you cook?'

'Kaz cooks.'

'Kaz, what do you think of this?'

'Well, it was just . . . a few first thoughts.'

'Is she a good cook?'

'Fabulous cook. She could be on the TV, she's that good.'

Turning to Kaz: 'How would you cook an oyster?'

'I wouldn't,' says Kaz. He nods approval.

'You cook. And you would like the kitchen laid out like this?'

'Well, it's just a few ideas.'

He drains his glass.

'We will see. I shall return next Tuesday.'

Two and a half weeks later, François phones and says he will be round that evening.

'Well, we were planning to . . .'

'I will see you at five.'

At 6.15 François arrives. He has a clipboard and a drawing on it. He leads us to the kitchen area.

'This is what you will do. Cooker here, dishwasher here, breakfast partition and worktops here. We will recess the freezer, fridge and a cupboard for *déchet* here, taking the space from the utility room and not the kitchen. These are the tiles I have chosen for you, and the sink will be . . .' he flicks though a brochure, '*comme ça*, and the cooker will be . . .' he flicks though another brochure, '*comme ça.*'

We sit down and look at it.

'A couple of questions?' I ask.

'Of course. Perhaps over a glass of wine?'

'Of course.'

'Can we have this colour wood for the prep areas?'

'Show me. Ah yes. That will be fine, but I must seal them with four coats of varnish.'

'And the tiles. As you say, but with perhaps a little texture, and cream not white?'

'*Texture bon, crème non.*'

Kaz and I look at each other. It was actually terrific. Recessing into the utility room was genius.

'Thank you, François, that's great.'

'*Bien sûr.* This is what I do. I can begin in perhaps four maybe five months.'

'Goodness, that's a long time. Not earlier?'

'Well, let me think. Next week perhaps?'

'That would be excellent if you could . . .' He's giggling.

'Next week. Ha ha ha. *Non non non.* I am an *atelier*. Do I look like I am not in demand? I have a job in the Auvergne for three months. Then I will call, and we will make a date. This is not London.'

Four, or maybe five, months later, François was back to supervise the delivery of the cooker. 'I will come to supervise the delivery of the appliances,' he had said on the phone.

'No, that's not necessary I'll take care of that.'

'Am I building you a kitchen?'

'Well, yes, of course, but . . .'

When the cooker came, he was on hand. Two big guys manhandled it into the living room and asked me to sign a paper saying it was delivered and in good condition. François was not about to let that happen. There was a stand-off, with voices raised and much shrugging of shoulders and insistence from François that they had better unpack it so we could see it was what we had paid for and check that it was in pristine condition. They, on the other hand, had other deliveries to make. François suggested that had they not stopped for breakfast then they wouldn't be in such a rush. Without the signed paper they had no choice but to unpack it, which took about a tenth of the time of the argument of whether they should unpack it or not. When all was revealed, François went to work. He was like a NASA engineer inspecting the next Mars lander.

'What's this?'

The two delivery men simultaneously squatted to inspect a blemish on the side of the stainless steel. One of them licks his finger and rubs it away and turns to his mate in triumph. François moves on. Suddenly he stands upright. 'What's that?' He points, and again the two chaps bend down. They stand, slightly pale. I walk over to look. It's dented. About a half centimetre of a dent, right at the bottom of the panel.

This will not do. This will not stand. François is now in full outrage mode on behalf of his halfwit client, me. I don't understand a word but I'm getting the drift that they can take it away and get another one delivered immediately. '*Immédiatement!*' Hands and shoulders go up from the chaps, palms and arms up towards the offending article. It's not going to happen, '*trois mois*' minimum.

By this time, the delivery chaps are seriously pissed off. They are looking at their watches. Then their phones come out, numbers are dialled and head office is called. They pace around the living room with François tapping his foot, arms folded. They come off the phone; more unintelligible French. François says something; they get back on the phone. They get off the phone and back to François. By this time, I'm completely confused. Then François turns to me.

'They don't speak English. They are from Marseille. They

hardly speak French. I have negotiated a 15 per cent discount. The bump will not be seen as it will be against the wall. You agree?'

'Well, er, sure.'

'*Bon!* says François. 'OK,' he says to the chaps. We all shake hands. The minus 15 per cent is written on the invoice, initialled, and I sign. Hands are shaken, and they are on their way.

François is stern. 'My apologies. They think because we don't live in the city we are stupid.'

A couple of months later, when François started work, he outlined his hours. He would finish precisely at midday for lunch, returning precisely at 1.30, and end his day at precisely 4.00. Or 4.30. Or 3.30 if he had to get some parts from Bricoman in Béziers. The first day he was back from lunch at 1.40 and not happy.

'How was lunch?

'Not good. Not good at all.'

'Oh, sorry to hear that. What was the problem?'

'The food was just acceptable. The wine was also acceptable. I can cope with acceptable. But it took thirty-four minutes to bring the first course. Thirty-four minutes. This is unacceptable. They know my hours. I told them my hours. But it took thirty-four minutes. This is not at all acceptable. We will try again tomorrow, and if it is still not acceptable then we have a problem.'

Tomorrow came.

François left for lunch at midday. François returned at 1.30.

'How was lunch'

'We have a problem.'

'Oh dear, anything I can do?'

'This is a serious problem which I have to address.'

'Did you mention it to them?'

'Yes. We agreed I would not be returning tomorrow, or ever again and I shall have to inform my fellow workers.'

'So there's no reprieve?'

'No. I have had a number of these problems. One I have not been back to for twenty years.'

The local village *bulletin municipal* is called *L'Echo des Garrigues* and is issued a couple of times a year. Essentially it tells you when to put the bins out, births, deaths and marriages, names of councillors, post office hours, a poem or two from a local bard, complete financial accounts of the village and an editorial by the Mairie. This editorial is usually a round-up of what's happening: things to take into account and a few lines reminding everyone about how precious our community is. One year, though, there was a rather stern rebuke. It reminded everyone, in pretty stark terms, to be polite and welcoming to incomers – the second-home owners. He sharpened his pen writing that they (we) were putting money into the village, that they (we) were buying the old houses they did not want and were doing them up using, by and large, local labour. It also reminded their readers that this was their village and that they were bound to abide by the rules and look after the place.

Over the years *L'Echo des Garrigues* had noted many complaints about the lack of parking spaces. This is a sore point in France. If you have a car then it's your right to park it as close to your house as physics will allow. There never seem to be enough parking spaces in Causses. They knocked down a couple of beautiful 'derelict' medieval houses for a car park for an additional twelve cars, but there still weren't enough, and people were constantly disrespecting the no entry sign to the Place Jules Milhau. Sometimes there were half a dozen cars and vans jammed in.

I woke up one morning recently to a revving of engines and a bumper-car dance of backing up and driving forwards, trying to get out of the medieval arch, which for even a middle-sized modern car has not much clearance. I watched the entertainment with a croissant and a coffee. After they had all left, I went down and found a note, flapping across the square. It was from the Mairie saying if this car is not moved then the police in Murviel would be called, and the owner would be fined and the car towed away. The words were rather blurred. It was a photocopy of a photocopy of a photocopy. I looked at it a little closer. At the top there was a date: April 2001.

8

Empty Attic

Vide-grenier – Pinkie Beaumont Mercedes-Farquharson – big business, small business – CHEZ NOUS – the linen conundrum solved – a chandelier

We needed to deck out the old place. The problem was, we were absolutely skint. But the French have the answer.

Vide-greniers are an obsession in rural France – not to be confused with *sous vide*, which are an obsession of chefs with too much time on their hands. *Vide-greniers* are open-air bric-a-brac markets that pop up on car parks and village streets from May to September. *Vide-greniers* can be translated as 'empty attics' (as opposed to *sous vide* which can be translated as empty wallet) and are the equivalent of yard sales in America, car boot sales in the UK and, in that other country called Paris, flea markets. They are an excuse for a day out, a chat with your mates, lunch on a deckchair. Don't be fooled into thinking this is a place of commerce. Selling is nice but not important. This is just as well, because 50 euros for an old toothbrush and 100 euros for a bike with no front wheel are not going to create a queue.

France is a place that finds it hard to applaud business success. Corporations, in the Anglo-Saxon sense, are regarded as a little gauche. French presidents have never been fans of Anglo-Saxon traditions of entrepreneurship. For the simple reason they are not French. The modern French terror is being subsumed by the English-speaking world. Much like the Scots.

Small local businesses with a dynasty are respected, as are

small start-ups. But actually starting up is a nightmare. Try getting a bank loan for a business. They present you with a Gordian knot, bind your hands and whip out a stopwatch. You have to jump through hoops to even get a bank account. And woe betide if you go overdrawn, even by a euro, which is good in some ways. It keeps household debt lower than in, say, the UK or America and makes people less blasé about money in general. But the downside is that it encourages people to stay small and play the system. France is a society of rules. *Ce sont les règles*. But those rules are for someone else, not you.

We had to get a couple of tyres on the car replaced one August so went to the local equivalent of KwikFit, in Thézan. We waited for half an hour, during which time Joe McVey, who had done the initial building work at 1 Place de l'Eglise, happened by for the same thing. That was lucky, since doing these sorts of things in Duolingo translation is not really nuanced enough. Ordering the correct rear tyres from a huge selection of radials and crossplys – OK, I don't know what I'm talking about but you get the picture – is a nightmare even in English. All of this requires a bunch of French colloquialisms and technical jargon. I gave it a go before Joe arrived, and the assistant lady looked at me as if I'd just asked to take the owner's wife to dinner, which I may have indeed done. This was a branch of a national chain run by locals, so you have the perfect blend of two cultures: the national chain mentality, '*l'ordinateur a dit non*', and the local staff who within minutes had become my relatives. The tyres on our car were so bad that big business said I couldn't drive it and that it would take at least a week to get the right ones. Had I got someone who could pick me up? Well, no, I live in Causses-et-Veyran and needed a car. 'Causses! Ah! How is Monsieur Baro? And Patrick! Does he still have that piece of land in the garrigue where he holds parties? How is

René? And Sebastian? The harvest was good for him last year?'
The manageress arrived. She spoke no English. But she shook
Joe's hand and they had a conversation. 'This is Brigitte, She's
in charge. She says you can borrow her car for a few days.'

'What?'

'She says she can ask her husband to collect her and you
can borrow her car.'

The next thing we knew, a young fellow no more than eighteen, but with a big thick beard, tattoos and a huge smile, led us to
a very serviceable little Peugeot. He introduced himself as Claude.
'A good French name,' I joked. I think he replied something along
the lines of he would grow into it, but his accent was so thick he
could have been saying 'I'll grow into a broad bean.' Off we went
in the boss's car, which we had for three days, no charge. Claude
still gives me a wave when we pass on the way to SuperU.

In France inherited wealth – we are talking castles and titles here –
is fine. It has the heady whiff of luck and condescension. Being
born well deserves congratulation. Which is odd, since the aims of
the Revolution enshrined in the 'Declaration of the Rights of Man
and of the Citizen' in 1789 are still held up as the shining banners
of French society. Among them is the end of social hierarchy to be
achieved by economic and legal equality. Nothing to argue with
there. Except in between then and now is Napoleon Bonaparte.
Napoleon solidified many of these revolutionary principles. In
fact, he decided they were so good that they should be shared
with extreme prejudice with the rest of the continent – six million
dead, one million of whom were French. Napoleon remains one
of the great dividers of French sensibilities. On the plus side he
introduced the State Council, the legal system, the administration
system and the Bank of France – all of which are still pillars
of the state. On the minus side he reintroduced slavery in the

French colonies and, by removing women's individual rights, he is regarded as French history's misogynist-in-chief. Which is interesting, since 'citizens', as in 'Declaration of the Rights of Man and of the Citizen', could only be men. His plusses are a bulwark of the political right and his minuses a bulwark of the political left. French love the philosophy of these things. This led to Napoleon's constant misreading of the perfidious British. He thought they were ready to emerge from under the boot of the monarchy and the aristocracy purely because it made sense on any scale of individual self-worth. What's more, the French had already done it, so it must be the right thing for everybody. On that basis he reasoned that oppressed peasants, from Cornwall to Culloden, would flock to him if he invaded. So he sold off the 825,000 square miles of French American territory to the US (the Louisiana Purchase) for $15 million, which he used to finance the preparations for the invasion of Britain. Insanely, though characteristically as a counterintuitive Anglo-Saxon country, the $15 million was lent by Barings Bank with the permission of the British government, who reckoned that the lesser of two evils was the US owning the territory rather than the overtly hostile French. Napoleon just couldn't understand that, within weeks of Mad George III saying he personally would lead his people against that nasty frog Boney, 280,000 men had volunteered to follow him. There was certainly a little disquiet in Britain as well. Some aristocrats thought that it might not be an altogether good thing that the establishment had just armed 280,000 hairy-arsed peasants.*

* History could have been very different. In 1785, the sixteen-year-old second lieutenant Napoleon Bonaparte from Corsica was training at the Ecole Militaire in Paris. Looking for adventure, he applied to join a scientific expedition to the Pacific led by Jean-François de Galaup, comte de La Pérouse. The young cadet was shortlisted but ultimately did not make the cut. The entire expedition was lost off the coast of Australia four years later.

Swinging back. If you really do have to earn money in France, then, for kudos and status, become a writer, artist or for preference a philosopher. At a pinch become a bureaucrat and join the political gravy train. In Britain or America or, come to think about it anywhere other than France, becoming an accountant, a banker, a marketing executive (whatever that is) is a life aim. In the UK, take an HND in Business Studies from Hendon Polytechnic and become CEO of a multinational and you will be regarded as an expert on everything.

'What do you want to be when you grow up, Pierre?'

'A philosopher.'

'Bravo, my boy. Here's a pipe, tweed suit and the address of a good lawyer.'

Vide-greniers are a great place to buy bric-a-brac to pep up a house. You see the same people year after year selling at *vide-greniers*. Buy something, anything, and they really do remember you and greet you heartily even a year or two later. Well, you would if someone paid you 50 euros for an old toothbrush and 100 euros for a bike with no front wheel. Or indeed 62 euros for a lovely tangerine-orange glass soda siphon from the 1930s, because it has the name R. Capiton, a long-defunct café from Béziers and the words 'Bièrres & Boissons Gazeuses' etched into it.

Yes, OK, OK.

I love it. I tried to track down R. Capiton. It's still serving, but only in the mists of time.

The problem with buying *trucs* (stuff) in the local markets is you'll always have in the back of your mind that your house might turn into one of those style sections in the Sunday newspapers edited by Pinkie Beaumont Mercedes-Farquharson (or Pinkie Beaumont and Mercedes Farquharson, I can never quite fathom). These are the crazy people who commission features called 'Garden furniture under £10,000 you'll just fall in love with', 'Chairs to chill in for less than the cost of a 5 series BMW' and 'Has Farrow & Ball lost its mojo? Bespoke paint that won't break your Coutts bank account.' They are accompanied by interviews with their friends, who are 'creatives' and own bijou houses in the up-and-coming parts of France, where they make features of derelict walls (beautiful raw plaster), yellowing, flaking paint (ochre crackle-glaze by Jocasta Innes), broken floor tiles, woodworm and how to make your 'bolt hole' smell of lavender and honeysuckle soap. The reason these features talk a lot about candles and smells is that their second homes are left empty for six months of the year so they smell of drains and soot when they are opened up. There's also the obsession for strange foot-high capital letters made of plaster which spell out 'HOME' or better still 'CHEZ NOUS', old baguette-cutting guillotines, nineteenth-century coffee grinders (jammed up with rust) and chipped and preternaturally stained sinks.

In truth, Pinkie's gaff is falling to pieces. That's not a problem for Pinkie, who will have become accustomed to the 'girl from the village' cleaning up before she, and her nice husband Marcus and their lovely family, arrive. You remember them, the ones who paid two guineas for their Ryanair flights? Well, that was Pinkie and Marcus. For 50 euros the Dysoning will have been done, flowers will be in every room, and a bottle of champagne will be in the fridge, all grabbed from '8 à Huit' a couple of hours before ETA. The house will look chez Mrs Hinch for a week, but as sure as tomcats return to pee on a lavender bush, so will the sweet smell of sewage.

There are levels of *vide-grenier*. SuperU car park is your basic entry level – we could say your tier one, full of tchotchkes. These are the true empty attic sales, just stuff cleaned out for a day out. Then there is tier two, village *vide-greniers* that sprawl through the streets on a Sunday and have a bit more of a fête vibe going on. You'll see them advertised on posters pasted onto anything that's stationary from March onwards. Village *vide-greniers* have quite a few professional vendors who have better stuff and prices that are 'really not that bad'. There are crêpe stalls and the odd local *vigneron* offering samples for free and bottles to buy, and local *jeunesse dorée* carving the place up on their very loud, very low-powered motorbikes. There's a good one at Thézan on the way to Béziers and one on Saturdays in St Chinian. There are other places as well, of course, but you'll just encounter the same people with the same stuff doing the rounds, so pick one and you've seen them all.

Then there's the top tier, the proper jobs, like those at Pézenas and Béziers. Béziers is once a week on Tuesday morning and is small but a cut above. It's on Les Allées Paul Riquet in the centre of town overlooked by the Wes Andersonesque Béziers Theatre. Paul Riquet is not to be confused with Paul Ricard, who invented his eponymous pastis. Riquet is the chap who created the Canal du Midi, constructed between 1662 and 1681. Originally called the 'Canal Royal en Languedoc', it was renamed the Canal du Midi after the Revolution. It was quite a feat of engineering, costing so much money that it bankrupted Riquet and so much effort that it killed him. He had made a fortune by having the licence to collect salt tax for Louis XIV, and he and the king were keen to construct the canal so that they didn't need to transport goods around Spain to get from the Atlantic to the Mediterranean coast of France. It runs 240 kilometres from the Étang de Thau – where the oysters are grown – across to Toulouse, where it connects with the Canal de Garonne.

Béziers market is small, but the quality is good. The stalls always seem to be piled high with linen, if you are into that sort of thing. Lots of people in rural France used to collect linen. It gave them a taste of luxury but at a price they could afford. When their houses are cleared, bundles appear on market stalls, starched into boards, tightly folded, almost unused, as they were kept for best.

Pézenas is the market that gets the blood pumping. Every six months or so, there is a big antiques fair laid out like a *vide-grenier* but about as far from SuperU car park as Sotheby's is from an Oxfam shop. I should mention that Pézenas is absolutely not like L'Isle-sur-la-Sorgue. The Pézenas market still has some self-respect.

They close the whole town, with police stopping cars far enough out that it becomes like a football crowd all heading in the same direction. There are accordion players and those Peruvian pan-pipe groups that seem to attract hordes of dancing toddlers. Pézenas has lots of permanent small antique 'warehouses' forming the nucleus of the twice-yearly markets. There's great architectural salvage here as well. Expensive, mind, but good stuff.

So off we went to the *vide-grenier* to try and find things to Frenchify 1 Place de l'Eglise, but it was really difficult, as everything we saw and liked was a cliché of Pinkie proportions. So we started to just find stuff ourselves, which has the added bonus of everything having a story. And everything in 1 Place de l'Eglise really does have a story. The sink in the bathroom picked up from the New Forest was bought online. The lights in the living room are from a factory near Southampton. The huge mirror in the living room is from Leeds. I'm rather proud of the table on the terrace made from an old door from the bar into which I have recessed three eighteenth-century Delft tiles – an idea copied from a table at Le Lézard Bleu restaurant up in the mountains. One evening, the door appeared outside the bar propped up against the wall ready for the *déchet*. I asked the owner, René, if

I could have it, and we trooped it back with my dear friend Gail from America. I like to think of it as Gail's table.

Then there's the Flemish brass (I think it's brass, though it could be bronze) church chandelier. We had a call from old chums Stephen and Françoise. Françoise's parents were French Belgian and had moved to Dover, where Françoise was brought up. Her father collected antiques as a hobby, and some of the bigger stuff had ended up with her sister in Kent in a barn and she said she thought there was an old brass chandelier in among it but couldn't be sure. We could have it if we went down to collect. Excellent. We needed something to hang in the big space on the stairwell where the *pigeonnier* once was. We pootled down and were presented in the driveway with this huge chandelier. It was in a bit of a state. Black, with old wires all over it, the remnants of a rough conversion to electricity ages since. The crumbling plastic faux candle-holders were still lodged in candle cups, originally there to catch the wax, but now horribly drilled to let the wire through. The story is it came from a church and was in this state when her father had bought it decades ago. The top of the chandelier below the hook where the chain would be attached is a Madonna with the Christ Child in one arm and the other arm held up with the palm out. As I say, it was black, and the wires were tarnishing the brass. It was in a sorry state. It weighs a ton, and we managed to just about get it into the back of the car. Back home, I manoeuvred it into the spare room, stood back and thought, blimey . . . I should just bin this.

I circled it, prodding it with a metaphorical stick for a few days, and then thought I had better dive in and wrestle it to the floor. I first snipped off all the wires and pulled out the crumbly fake candles still holding the old bulbs. Getting close up, I could see that there were little brass pins holding each of the twelve arms, and on each there was a number corresponding to a number on the central column. I tapped the pins and each arm came free, and the cup and candle holder unscrewed smoothly. A couple of hours later, it was laid out like an Airfix kit. The Madonna and Child are beautifully made. I had a fiddle, and blow me if the babe unscrews, as does the hand and arm. Here again precision made. It will turn only until the babe is in the right position.

Now the messy bit. I had searched on the interweb and found that the way to clean it was to fill a plastic washing-up bowl with salt and vinegar and make a paste. It was like mixing nerve gas. The fumes were awful. Nothing like the tincture of Walkers crisps I had convinced myself it would be. I buried three of the arms in it and retired for a couple of hours. When I returned, it was a miracle. Not as in loaves and fishes. Much better than that. Underneath the black was beautiful golden-coloured metal, dull but after a bit of elbow grease and Brasso up it came like sunshine in the palm of my hand. I was amazed. It took a week or so to get the whole thing cleaned and back together. And I mean a week almost full time. And about 10 kilos of salt and at least 5 litres of vinegar. It took months for the black to wear off my hands. It took Kaz a couple of days in to suggest to me, as if talking to a five-year-old, that a pair of rubber gloves might be a good idea. But there it was, this magnificent chandelier. Glorious. The only annoyance was the drilled holes in the cups.

By then I was intrigued and did a bit of digging round. Apparently these types of chandeliers were characteristic of those made in Dinant in Belgium from the fifteenth century onwards – you can see one in the background of Jan Van Eyck's *The Arnolfini Portrait*, in form at any rate – that one is more ornate. They have been made there ever since, certainly into the twentieth century. I sent a photo to a dealer in Holland. It appears our one was made in the mid- to late nineteenth century, probably a bespoke commission for a Catholic church – given the Madonna and whatnot. The big brass sphere on the bottom is there to reflect the light around from the candles.

It now hangs at eye level when you stand at the top of the stairs before you turn into the *grenier*. François the builder put it up. He said it was one of the worst jobs he had ever had to do. I've got white candles in it, and the Madonna looks very happy in her new home. The dealer also gave an unsolicited auction estimate, which was eye-watering. I was flabbergasted. I phoned Françoise and Stephen and told them that they had better have it back. Of course, they said no. I can imagine it hanging there until the place falls down.

9

A Storm and the Sky

Morning – a beautiful day – the oddness of hardware – an evening before the mast – sunsets over the mountains – the Perseids – Moon

We had not the slightest idea a storm was on the way. The sky was as blue as it had been for weeks; the breeze was quiet and friendly. Maria at the local shop had chatted at me that morning as I bought bread. I think she had said something about rain, but I had grinned as I always do and nodded and mumbled '*Oui*', '*Vraiment?*' or some such. I still haven't got my brain around her accent – or half her vocabulary, truth be told. I pottered round past the bar and bonjoured the Old Gentlemen's Club, who were strategically camped as always on the corner so they could intimidate the traffic from whatever end of the village it approached. They wished me good morning and looked to the sky. I looked with them and smiled without a clue what they were looking at or saying. I imagine it's something along the lines of 'Next time, let's point at the road and talk about the state of the Russian economy.' I swung round and back through the arch and bumped into Derek and Maureen. They had bought the Old Bakery the year before, a massive and daunting restoration job. We had consoled them when they showed us their botched roof terrace, the result of a bad builder. They did all the work themselves, apart from tanking the terrace, and had got a good deal of kudos around the village for their tenacity. They were working in the *cave* when

I walked up; they stopped and came out covered in brick dust. They were always covered in brick dust.

'Seems to be a buzz in the village today,' I said.

'Something about rain later?' they suggested.

I peered into the sky. 'Looks OK to me. Going swimming this afternoon.'

They suggested we meet for a drink sometime and I ambled off down Rue des Porches.

It was our first stay after the building work to get two floors habitable and we had been living at 1 Place de l'Eglise for a just few days. We hadn't yet quite figured out how much of the domestic stuff operated. The immersion heaters seemed to be on all the time and the taps seem to pour hot and cold as they suited, no matter how much one played with them.

Newcomers don't realize the little nuances in how domestic items work from one country to another. Take our bathroom sink, for example. It's got one tap on it and one nozzle. If you turn it on slightly then cold water comes out at full rush, but the mystery of wherefore hot remains. You hold your hands under for thirty seconds and it's still cold. Wait another minute and it's colder still. Turn the tap further and the cascade of water stays the same. It's not until your hands get scalded that you realize you have in fact no control over the flow, you are just adjusting the heat, that the penny drops. It's the same with things like window catches and door locks and whatnot. At the time you just think we'll figure it out. Then, when the weather turns, that's not such a good idea.

Throughout the day, the temperature remained in the thirties. The sky began to change colour unnoticed. To the north, clouds were banking up behind a line so straight it might have been drawn with a vast ruler. We thought nothing of it and spent the day at the river. By six the clouds were still behind the line, and we continued to think nothing of it as we prepared and ate supper and watched the sun go down and the bats pop out from the barn shutters opposite like black corks.

Some evenings, the Milhau Square bats stray into our bedroom, fluttering in circles, across the ceiling and around the bed. We switch off the light and let them settle hanging upside down on the beams. Then we creep close. Sometimes we get almost nose to nose in the moonlight. They just look quizzically for ten or twenty seconds. Their faces make me think of Pomeranian dogs. Then off they go, a black flash out of the window and away.

Some early summer evenings, before the bats awake, swifts, who nest under our guttering – there are so many some years I have heard 1 Place de l'Eglise called *lotissement de martinets* – miss their landing slot and career through the window and become frantic. Without bats' echo-location they get more and more confused and end up caught in the muslin curtains in the bathroom. I whisper to them as I untangle them, holding them firmly but gently until I have them free. They are exquisite up close. Tiny legs. Their Latin name is *Apus apus*, which derives from the Greek *a*, 'without', and *pous*, 'foot'. And their wings. So long they cover their whole body and half as much again. Scythe-shaped, as if from a fletcher's bench. A tiny beak and a huge mouth, literally a grin from ear to ear, used to catch insects on the wind. I walk gently to the window, open my palm and watch them go like a bullet. I feel exhilarated for days. How lucky. How many people even see a swift close up, never mind catch one?

As the evening drew into night, the darkness was so lovely we strolled into the vineyards and repaired to bed around midnight, the stars still twinkling. The air was heavy and hot, so I made sure that all the windows and shutters were open before I slid between the sheets, sighed and fell asleep immediately.

A moment later – two hours – a colossal bang echoed round the house. I leaped up, convinced an aircraft had landed on the roof.

'What the hell was that!'

A second crash, a flash of light, rain lashing the boards, wind howling through the shutters. I could hear bangs all over the house echoing across Jules Milhau and Eglise. More lightning, more crashing, great thumps as loose shutters banged in the wind. Kaz was up and out the door to make sure the children were OK. I shoved my head back under the covers. Then I heard George shouting at the top of his voice, 'I can't shut the doors!' I ran up the stairs to find the *grenier* awash. George was leaning on the doors that led out onto the roof terrace to keep them closed and water was cascading through the gap at the bottom.

'They're supposed to bloody well close!' I hollered.

'Well, I can't see how to close them.'

'Let me have a look,' I shouted. As George moved aside, the doors flew open, and half an airborne river threw itself at me. In an instant I found myself in the same position as George five seconds before: my back holding the doors shut with a torrent thundering across the floor and down the stairs.

'Get that stone and wedge the thing shut.' I shouted. I held the torrent at bay as George eventually managed to get a stone in place, but it still wouldn't close fully and still water flooded through.

'The bloody catch must be broken.' I looked up and across the *grenier*. Water was pouring in under the pantiles. The storm was right above us. No gap between lightning and thunder. How great was this? I was soaked and grinning from ear to ear.

We were in a force ten off the Cape. 'Damn it all, man! Look lively there!' I shouted in a rather poor impression of Russell Crowe as Captain Aubrey.

'Oh, for God's sake!' howled George with disgust as water showered round him. I could see his point. His bed was about to float away.

A minute or so later, I had managed to wedge a couple more stones against the door, and the torrent had been reduced to a trickle, but it was by no means watertight. I picked my way down the wet stairs to see what was happening in the rest of the lake we called home. Kaz and Freya had managed to get all the shutters closed but not before almost everything had been soaked. The tempest was still howling outside, but there was now little else to be done.

George took up residence in the downstairs bedroom and we all decided the best thing to do was to wait it out. Slowly the storm moved away, the rain ebbed, the lightning and thunder flashed and grumbled away over the mountains, and I eventually dozed off.

I woke with a start. Blimey. I remembered the mayhem and staggered out of bed and opened the shutters. Sunshine flooded in, and wonderful, warm, musty, damp air followed. I leaned out and looked up and down Jules Milhau. It was as dry as a bone. I wandered out into the hallway, and a small, rapidly reducing damp patch was all the evidence of our flood. I walked up the stairs to the *grenier*. The floor was completely dry. I opened the doors on the roof terrace and the light was soft and bright, and not a spot of water to be seen. I examined the recalcitrant window latch, thinking I'd have to get someone over to fix it. I fiddled and in doing so noticed that it not only opened by pulling the handle down but if you pushed it went up as well. That's odd. I had another go. It suddenly dawned on me that the door wasn't broken at all. To lock it you just had to push the handle up and to open it push the handle down. Now you wouldn't know that, would you, if all your reference points were locks and handles made in Sheffield?

Around Causses, the weather can be some of the most extreme in France. It has not only the hottest summers, but also the highest winds. It has spectacular lightning storms – our encounter had been kids' stuff, we learned later – hailstorms that can strip a car of its paint ('strip a car of its paint' seems to be a phrase used a good deal around here) and occasional floods. A couple of years before we arrived in September 2002, 27 inches of rain fell in one day and caused severe flooding. A dam burst, killing more than twenty people, flooding vineyards and ruining the vines. It's now pretty common, flooding, particularly in St Chinian. We were treated to a snowstorm in 2018. About 5 inches fell in a morning, and we made snow angels in the car park and sipped hot wine in the bar; by the afternoon it had gone, as if never there.

Sunsets are precious. They come and go in ten minutes or less. But catch one after a hot day when there are high clouds puffing over the mountains then the sky is set ablaze. Fierier than the fieriest science-fiction sky, viscid, moving moment by moment, mellifluous ambers and reds and crimsons and yellows against a sapphire sky which gradually goes black. Then the stars appear, as close to a Sahara night as I am likely to witness. There is no light from the ground. The stars appear above the treetops and arc over in a great, black, sparkling bowl: Orion, Great and Little Bear, Arcturus, Betelgeuse, Sirius, Rigel, Vega, Capella, Canopus, Procyon, Mars and Venus and Saturn. More stars than there are grains of sand.

Early to mid-August evenings are the best of the best. Then, celestial sparklers entertain us. The Perseids have been a feature of my life for thirty years since we first went to Provence to stay with Anne. We would stand on her terrace, the stage the vast expanse of the Luberon, as streaks of stardust scored the black night, sometimes tens in a minute, some coming in so flat they lasted seconds and sliced open the sky from Roussillon to Apt.

Now we lie on our terrace looking up. Sometimes there are none, sometimes a few. Now and again, the sky lights up as if God has thrown iron filings in a cosmological fire.

One spring night a year or two ago, I woke. Through the wide-open bedroom window shone a white light. I was confused, I sat up and, as sleep left me, I realized it was a magnesium moon, the brightest, super-trooper moonbeam I had ever seen. I rose and walked into it like a pilgrim for the stars, squinting, looking up at this huge, stunning, gibbous disc. I breathed in the light. It was so clean, so clear, so cleansing it seemed the right thing to do. Then I walked back and gently woke Kaz. 'Look at the moon,' I said. I took her hand, and in the spotlight we swayed sleepily.

Later, as her breathing steadied and she slept again, I whispered: 'Come a little bit closer, hear what I have to say.

Let's go dancing in the light,

We know where the music's playing,

I want to see you dance again,

Because I'm still in love with you.'

And then I sobbed, just a little, for my happiness and for my sadness.

10

Bienvenue

La Mouche – Cébenna, la Femme allongeé – Olargues – les
Petetas de Murviel – Mas des Dames – lunch

On your way down to visit us, there's a moment on the road when you'll know you've arrived.

Having negotiated Béziers, you'll be looking for the D154, Route de Corneilhan, marked to Murviel. You'll swing past La Ferme Biterroise on the right – Biterrois is the name of Béziers folk – and a kilometre or so further, on your left, you'll pass two tall signs, one for La Mouche – not to be confused with the name of the French remake of Phoebe Waller-Bridge's *Fleabag*, which is not great, though it does star the brilliant Camille Cottin from the series *Call My Agent!* (*Dix pour cent*) – and the other for olive oil 'Domaine Pradines le Bas'. When you've been here a day or two, we'll take you to La Mouche, the sort of art studio you'd find on Cork Street in London but not as a rule in a provincial part of France. As they say themselves: 'Three exhibition rooms and a sculpture park, in the heart of an olive grove and an oil mill. La Mouche is a place where nature and culture come together.' If there's a launch party for an exhibition, we'll go blag an invite. Wear your good shoes and best suit or frock: you'll be mingling with the beau monde of Béziers. If contemporary art is not your thing, then there's always the olive oil: pricey but sublime. It's a shame that Corinne is not there any more. She knew her olive oil and she was well up on the art scene. Thankfully she's not gone far. She is now at Domaine de

Météore, near Causses, which grows vines inside the crater of a meteor which struck the hillside thereabouts some 10,000 years ago. She's running their restaurant, 'The Crater at Domaine du Meteore', with her chef partner Nicholas Delorme. I'm told it's good. We should go.

Drive past La Mouche, and a couple of kilometres later, after a right curve, there in front of you is the Montagne Noire range rising straight out of the plain. Don't try and look this up on Street View. It's a real disappointment. You'll not resist a peek, but it won't impress. You have to be there. As John Steinbeck said of Californian redwood trees: 'The redwoods, once seen, leave a mark or create a vision that stays with you always. No one has ever successfully painted or photographed a redwood tree.' I always get that same feeling when I crest the brow of that hill and the plain – *là-bas* – is laid out before me.

There's a layby just after the curve, and you might want to take a moment. To the right is the classic French village of Corneilhan, a hill surrounded by ancient houses and on its peak a church. I visited Brittany when I was about eighteen with my best school chum, Martyn Grayer, who was the funniest and brightest of us. We ended up in a bar with some French girls. I was the quiet one, trying to be sophisticated and ending up just being boring. Matt – we called him Matt Emulsion because he earned money decorating during the holidays – was chatting away and asked one of the girls, who spoke pretty good English, where she came from. 'A little village in Brittany called . . . you won't have heard of it.'

Matt didn't miss a beat. 'Oh yes, I know the one, with the lovely Norman church in the square on the top of the hill.'

She was utterly beguiled. 'Oh, how wonderful. You know it!'

'Of course,' said Matt, 'the post office just down from the bar?' She was smitten.

Later, I asked how on earth did he know that village. He looked at me with pity. 'Every small French village has a church on a hill and a square and bar and a post office.'

To the left on a clear day you can see the Pyrenees, with Mont Canigou white-topped between the clouds. Look carefully right in front of you, lying between the peaks of the Caroux, the most southerly part of the Cévennes, you'll see what looks like a colossal body lying flat, face to the stars. This is Cébenna, '*la Femme allongée*', shaped from the mountains that climb above Olargues, one of the most beautiful, and probably my favourite, village in France (not that I've visited them all for comparison, you understand). Evenings at Olargues are precious. I never want to leave. Its stunning feature is the Pont du Diable, the Devil's Bridge, an astonishingly delicate medieval construction. An arch that hardly seems to dare stay standing, but so it has for 800 years. The wise burghers of Olargues have left the bridge just as it was built, so no railings. When I stand at its crest and look down 30-odd metres to the river Jaur, it gives me the willies. The river pools are packed with fish, herons drift in to dine, a sharp eye might catch the flash of Tyndall blue as a kingfisher flits downstream, settling on a branch by the bridge for a moment and then heading on for supper. Lift your head, and above you is the bell tower, so often in early summer buzzed by a swarm of swifts so high they look like gnats.

From Olargues, Cébenna's head can be seen through the trees as nothing more than a jagged outcrop, but from the Rue de Corneilhan it really does look spookily like a colossal prone body weathered from the white gneiss rock. The legend of Cébenna is one of the great stories of the Languedoc. Legends have many lives. This is my favourite. It takes a piece of Greek myth and squeezes in a local twist:

In a time before our time when Zeus was battling the Titans, Héric and Cébenna, weary of the war, left the fight and found refuge in the Caroux, where they fell in love. There they lived quietly and secretly. One day, Héric was fishing in the Mediterranean Sea and was swept away by a mysterious current until he was eventually washed up on the shores of Greece. There he was captured by Zeus, who forced him to fight with the Gods against the Titans and he was killed in battle. Cébenna spent every moment pining for her lost love, waiting by the seashore, overcome with sorrow. When he did not come home, she returned to the mountains to rest, where she lay down and eventually fell asleep, weeping tears that still flow to this day down the Gorges d'Héric.

When we go to Olargues, we'll take you to dinner at the Fleurs d'Olargues, facing the bridge. I'll book a table in the garden overlooking the allotment where they grow all their own veg. It's run by a Danish family, two generations. The elderly mum is wonderful. A couple of years ago we were the last four before they closed for the winter. We asked for the bill, and she joined us. Perfect English, naturally, and dressed, as all good chatelaines should, to kill. If the Fleurs d'Olargues hasn't got a Michelin star by the time you visit, then we'll make banners and protest outside.

Back on the Béziers Road, you are now passing Thézan and then a long drag past SuperU to Murviel. On an unprepossessing traffic island with the office de tourisme de pech (all lower case – very on point) on your right, stop off at the bakery on the left for three baguettes of Tradition – buy three and you get a fourth free. The place doesn't look much like a centre of baking excellence, but the bread is actually sensational.

On through Murviel, round the one-way, following the signs to Causses. If it's July then you'll be confronted by Les Petetas de Murviel. On balconies and at traffic islands, by the roadside and tucked into doorways, are life-size straw dolls variously dressed as tradespeople from the first half of the twentieth century. There's a lot of effort goes into it, but they all look a little creepy to me. You'd think it is a tradition that's been going on for centuries, but in fact the whole thing was dreamed up in 1997. Fair play, we all need an edge in the tourist trade, but I'm not sure there's a Disney deal in the offing any time soon.

Murviel is a true *circulade* village, almost completely intact. Send a drone up and there it is, an ovoid, the outer walls now outer houses and the rest of the town packed in like a log store. At the centre is the church next to the chateau at the top of the hill. The name Murviel comes from *murs*, walls, and an archaic spelling of *vieux*, old. It's the perfect place to build a fortified stronghold with views of the plain right down to the Mediterranean and up to the mountains behind.

Follow the road past the Salon Jean Moulin and then the signs to Causses-et-Veyran, ignore the *Autres Directions*, and go on past the cemetery on the right. Round the corner and you burst back into the countryside, then it's down the hill following the signs to a vineyard called Mas des Dames at the bottom.

Why it's called Mas des Dames – which translates rather limply to 'Estate of the Ladies' – is a bit of a question. It's not, as you might think, because it's run by a group of ladies – although it kind of is. There are two popular explanations. The first is that before Lidewij van Wilgen bought the *domaine* in 2002, three generations of the previous owners had only daughters. The second is that Lidewij has three daughters who grew up on the estate and are now involved in the winemaking. Whatever, there's some sort of tangled nominative

determinism going on here. It's one of those names that just has to be.

Lidewij, the owner, wrote a book about buying Mas des Dames called *The Domain: A Woman, an Old Vineyard, a New Life* (available only in Dutch) a story straight out of the Hollywood plot book: woman at the height of her high-flying career thinks there's more to life, buys a vineyard in the south of France and after much travail finds true happiness. It's a cliché, but that's exactly what she did. She was thirty-two, director of strategy at Saatchi's in Amsterdam, married to a copywriter and with a new baby. I don't know what it is about advertising people that they all want to own vineyards. Sir John Hegarty of Bartle, Bogis and Bean – he the fellow who came up with the slogan *Vorsprung durch Technik* for Audi, among much else – owns a vineyard called Hegarty Chamans just over the hills near Carcassonne. Anyway, Lidewij – I'm being presumptuous here as I don't really know her – buys Mas des Dames and, using her advertising chops and after studying wine-making in Montpellier, twenty years later she's a top Euro wine-maker, selling her wares all over the place with fans like Jancis Robinson and Gordon Ramsay. The wines are labelled under Terre-Des-Dames and are rather wonderfully called variously La Dame, La Diva, La Diva Rosé, La Diva Blanche, L'Unique. Her wine is pretty hard to get unless you visit, so I'm expecting by now you have loaded up a couple of cases of La Dame and La Diva and are back on the road to Causses.

Carry on driving, and up ahead you get another part view of Cébenna lying in among the Montagne Noire, then across a narrow bridge, the hills now turning into mountains. Soon, to the left, you'll see a sign to Veyran, the site of the house of the eponymous centurion. We'll go there another time, since you'll be getting a little peckish, and we promised you late lunch, and that stop at Mas des Dames took a little longer than planned.

So it's on to Causses. As you progress, you'll come into the bottom of the village past the Roman pillars and then past the Causses-et-Veyran sign (also in Occitan 'Cauces E Vairan'), sweep round to the right at the bar and then into Place de la Pompe Neuve, née Place du Marché. We'll be there to greet you. Oh, and don't forget, a bottle from those two cases of Terre-des-Dames wouldn't go amiss for lunch.

11

A Time to Keep Silence

Patrick Leigh Fermor – in the footsteps of ghosts – the
quality of silence – a time to listen – the joy of nothing

By the time I bent down to read the polished brass nameplate outside number 50 Albemarle Street I was convinced that inside the man with his name on the door was about to fire me. It was a fine summer morning. I was twenty-four years old. It was my first day, and I was horribly late.

Traffic clamoured in Piccadilly. A meter man prowled. A gent whistled a cab. A Jag drew up, and out hopped as pert a deb as 1982 could muster. I took a deep breath and as calmly as panic allowed negotiated the perfectly polished Burgundy-red Georgian door of John Murray Publishers. I announced myself at reception to a patrician lady in black who sat before the altar of a plug-in telephone exchange. She directed me to a sweeping staircase and the second floor. I climbed. Suddenly there he was on the landing above, wearing a tweed three-piece suit, bright red braces, topped out with a heavy damask plum bow-tie, one of many made for him, I learned much later, by Freya Stark from the curtains of her house when she moved from London to Asolo in 1946. He advanced. I stopped. Without a word he pushed into my hand a first edition of Paddy Leigh Fermor's *A Time to Keep Silence*. 'Mr Dolby! The new bug! Have you read it? I've decided you should read it!' Spritely as a teenager, although he was in his seventies then, he turned and was gone.

Not much more than a year later, Mr Murray introduced me to my future wife in a not too dissimilar manner.

It took me a month or so to learn that Lord Byron, Jane Austen, Charles Darwin, George Crabbe, Washington Irving, David Livingstone, Samuel Taylor Coleridge and John Murrays back to 1812 had climbed those same stairs, though in much more illustrious circumstances than I. The latest John Murray - number VI – was one of that small group of literary lions who went up to Oxford in the late 1920s, among them Poet Laureate Sir John Betjeman, cartoonist Osbert Lancaster and art historian Sir Kenneth Clark.

As he and I became familiar, Mr Murray (Jock to his friends) told me wonderful tales. His first job was to accompany the tall, handsome, then nearly blind Doctor Axel Munthe on his tour of the Mediterranean in 1930 promoting *The Story of San Michele*: Mr Murray's indenture to repel advances from the author's many female admirers. One cold day, as the inadequate heating banged and grumbled, he told me that while his aunt lay dying in an upstairs room – by then my boss's office – she incubated and hatched duck eggs to pass the time. Petitioning my opinion of the office chairs, he confided that he had cured Bernard Shaw's wife of lumbago with cabbage water – 'good for the back, bad for the breath'. One afternoon, he snuck up on me as I spied a famous author from the fifth-floor mezzanine. I had heard no approach, just felt a breath to my right. I turned slowly to find Mr Murray had fixed me with a stare from no more than a few inches. Before I could withdraw to my comfort zone, he laid his hand on my shoulder, leaned in a touch further and with the essence of command dared me to spit. The revelation followed that in his youth he could expectorate from this position through the 2-inch polished Cuban mahogany banister-gap down 60 feet onto any Homburg or bowler left on the marble-top parlour table in the vestibule below. Mr Murray was a stealthy man.

'I delighted in the Sherlock Holmes books,' he confessed to Naim Attallah not long before he died on a warm sunny Thursday, 22 July 1993, 'and in a way that was what first endeared me to authors. I was a schoolboy on my holidays, and my grandfather was ill. He said, "I think Sir Arthur Conan Doyle is calling today; will you be kind to him? I hope he may bring another typescript." Conan Doyle brought the last volume of the Sherlock Holmes stories, and I was so staggered by this distinguished man's courtesy to a young whippersnapper like me that I thought: if this is an author, let me spend my life with authors.'

Paddy Leigh Fermor's obituary of his much-loved lifelong friend appeared in the *Independent* the following Friday:

> 'It is hard to think of a more apt setting for him than No. 50 Albemarle Street, with its beautiful rooms, and portraits and books and cases of mementoes, and its mixture of archaic style and informality, of activity and unhurried leisure. The traditions of Byron's friendship with Jock Murray's ancestor played a great part in the life of No. 50, and the poet's spirit seems to pervade those rooms. Looking through typescript, then galleys then page proofs there with Jock was a great delight. Especially when they were tossed aside to make room for tea or sherry or whisky and soda, and Osbert Lancaster on the way back from drawing his daily caricature would wander in full of marvellous gossip; or Kenneth Clark with an armful of illustrations or John Betjeman with news of a new Early English discovery in some remote Fenland parish – could they talk about it with John Piper? (Betjeman and Jock shared an expert knowledge of campanology.)

Cannon Lodge, halfway between Hampstead Heath and a slender steeple, with its Keats'-eye view of all London, had a similar uncontemporary charm. At the end of a day of last-minute corrections, under one of the tall trees, or by a blazing fire, any of the above might come to dinner, or Freya Stark fresh from Asia Minor, Ruth Jhabvala from Rajasthan or Dervla Murphy from the Andes and, very often, Jock and Diana's favourite neighbour, Peggy Ashcroft.

Jock and Diana came several times to Greece, and it was a great surprise to discover that Jock was an accomplished tree surgeon: one glance at an ailing growth would send him shinning up into the branches and putting things most knowledgeably to right with saw, twine, bast and tar.

Five weeks ago, we were talking about the ravages of time that we noticed in ourselves and he said, halfway between a sigh and a laugh, 'Yes. Old age is not for sissies.' He confronted his own with great Stoicism, and leaves us all diminished.

I did as Mr Murray bade and read *A Time to Keep Silence*, and it became 'my book'. It tells of the author's stays in monasteries in France in the 1950s, principal among them the Carolingian abbey Saint-Wandrille de Fontanelle at Saint-Wandrille-Rançon in Normandy. Fermor's is an elegant story of a man who loves life and who comes to love it the more through the physical and emotional catharsis achieved by solitude and silence. He describes sitting in his cell for the first time, expecting to write immediately, the distractions of the world gone, only to find that after just an hour he is 'felled by the hammer-stroke of loneliness'. But as time passes, and the rhythms of ecclesiastical days absorb him, the accretions of his outside life fall away, and silence and simplicity reveal his world with uncluttered clarity.

Musician, composer, artist, writer and mushroom collector John Cage, in his famous 1950 talk 'Lecture on Nothing', tried to leave behind the notion of silence as an absence of sound: 'What we require is silence; but what silence requires is that I go on talking.' Listening to silence makes such sense that the opposite is true. Sound only exists because there is silence, we communicate only because there are words between silences. His much-maligned piece *4.33* is four minutes and thirty-three seconds of sounds the 'listener' receives during that time. It is the time that bounds the piece.

Carl Honoré, in his book *In Praise of Slowness*, suggests:

> The Slow philosophy is not about doing everything at a snail's pace, it's about seeking to do everything at the right speed. Savoring the hours and minutes rather than just counting them. Doing everything as well as possible, instead of as fast as possible. It's about quality over quantity in everything.

There are volumes written about silence. Silence, the need to wander, the comfort of fire, these things are as personal as thought and expression.

In summer at 1 Place de l'Eglise, sound defines the canvas of silence. Here is a world without urgent roar and rumble. No television to shout at me, no music played loud. My mother, who is ninety-five, sits in silence in her Derbyshire cottage and is happy. In London we all expect noise. But at 1 Place de l'Eglise we live by our own clock, not by that dictated by the sounds of other people's lives. We wake as and when, eat lunch at three, dinner at ten and sit and read and play games and talk into the hot night.

At 1 Place de l'Eglise the day begins with silence and sound. Our bedroom is dark; as for centuries, shutters fend off the sun in summer and exclude the cold and wind in winter. Before I open my eyes, I hear a gang of sparrows. Their frantic, scrapping chirrups are crisp and echo across Place Jules Milhau. When they are gone, I hear nothing but the rustle of cotton sheets, the sound of breathing. I pad downstairs to the kitchen. Bare feet on warm stone. The living room is dark. Silence ebbs and flows as my soles brush the *tommettes*. I brew hissing coffee.

It is June, the windows have been open all night. I crank and clank shutters, and the sun dashes in, followed slowly by warmth. I hear a woman's voice: '*Bonjour, messieurs-dames.*' It might be next door or a mile away. In Place de l'Eglise leaves on the honey locust rustle. A thousand years of commotion lie in the walls around me. Every stone might tell a story. Each tile and beam belongs to someone who placed it there. A man who then slept and ate that day and then the next and then the next until one day he stopped and was complete. The ancient walls make me a part of their story.

I make my way to the roof terrace. It is hot already. Clear and strong, the church clock clanks nine. Swifts wheel and scream, shooting into the sky, fast-moving dots, round and round the pantiled rooftops and are gone. Silence returns.

A dog barks in the mountains.

The rev of a car is just audible. Second by second, it grows louder, then peaks and fades. Quiet returns. I sit and listen to my thoughts. A vast iron door knocker bangs on dense old wood somewhere across the village. *Calades* magnify the sound to a boom.

Voices.

Then they are gone.

I sip my coffee in the warm and quiet and let an hour drift

by. Below in the house I hear sounds of stirring. Then the village tannoy: loud, tinny: '*Allo. Allo* . . .' announcing the fish man is in the Place du Marché, or there are boxes of peaches for sale, or the pizza man is due that evening. The difference in the sound of nothing makes the sound of something sharp and often cacophonous. Cars are consequential. People's voices become distinct, their owners known without sight or introduction. A clatter becomes colossal.

The family stirs, and voices, not loud, creep through the halls and stairwell. A shower hisses. I hear George rise from his bed in the *grenier*: he pads across the floor, down the stairs. Most mornings now I fancy I can hear the same.

I rise. A chink as I retrieve my cup from the marble-topped table. A hawk's cry cracks the air. I look up and watch a kestrel dart from horizon to horizon.

I dress, crunch croissant and make my way to our massive wooden blue front door. Opening it is an effort. Like an old man's body it creaks and moans. I haul it shut behind me.

Under the stone arch and into Jules Milhau. A tortoiseshell cat meows and slinks my legs. I stroke her. She purrs and pushes.

I walk through to the Place du Marché. Camille and her dog Manon are bustling to the car park. '*Bonjour, madame. Bonne journée.*' She hurries on. I walk slowly past the cemetery, my shoes crunching on gravel, then silent as the metalled road shades to weedy clay. Along the lane between blowsy fennel and a crumbling lichen-etched *mur de pierre*, to the horse paddock. An elderly mare gallops up. The ground rumbles. I rub her greying, musty, dusty nose then turn and amble on into the warming hills.

Cicadas test their wings.

A shrew nosing deeper for cool comfort rustles in the parched grass.

High above, a jet grumbles, etching the vast, perfect blue.

Later, the distant church clock strikes its tinny chimes; three minutes after, it repeats, as it has done for centuries, in case I, or workers in the vines, miss the first announcement.

Silence in the hills is full of sound. One morning, we drive to the mountains above St Nazaire de Ladarez, along lanes that, after miles, become white stone track, walled either side by packed-tight, scrubby holly oak. Turn off the engine and step out into the heat. *Garrigue* blankets the land. Shout into the *arrière-pays*, and there is no return. Below, in the valley, a convocation of eagles drifts and cries. In the undergrowth lie great mounds of formic ants.

Listen.

Twenty metres distant you can hear the rustle of their millions of feet. Run your hand over them and their acid-panic throws back your head, and the rustle becomes a reed broom stroking a barn floor.

In the air dragonflies as big as a boxer's hand burr by, cutting this way and that, round this tree and that bush, down out of sight, up, back. In French their name is as beautiful as their form: *libellule*.

In St Nazaire gardens you can hear the thrum of hummingbird hawk-moths darting from one lonicera trumpet to the next.

Sit.

You will hear water, and crickets, and randy frogs.

Silence may be bitter or sweet. Why are there so few words for silence? The cloistered silence of stone monasteries; the silence of a northern forest; the silence of two men sipping pints in a favourite boozer; the silence between longtime lovers; the silence at the end of a relationship; the silence of mourning; the silence of a house at 4 a.m. full and yet empty; the silence after an explosion, the spilt second before mayhem; the silence of a library; the silence of remembrance.

The young St Augustine, when a pupil of Aurelius Ambrose, Bishop of Milan, in the late fourth century, noted in his 'autobiography' *Confessions*, Book Six, Chapter Three, that when Ambrose read,

> his eyes scanned the page and his heart sought out the meaning, but his voice was silent and his tongue was still. Anyone could approach him freely and guests were not commonly announced, so that often, when we came to visit him, we found him reading like this in silence, for he never read aloud.

This was a curious observation. Ambrose had changed the meaning of the words 'to read'. Before Ambrose, and no doubt others who also read 'to themselves' but did not have their activities recorded, reading meant to read out loud – even in libraries, which to our shushing sensibilities must have been a rum affair.

Sound may be unnecessary, but what of sharing? Was the lack of sharing diminishing the potency of the words for the reader? Why indeed was it natural to read out loud? Was it a relic of the 'old' way of using words? Words were said, and their shared meaning created pictures in the listener's mind. The act of sharing was by speaking. Writings were commonly read aloud at that time and before, part of the oral tradition of storytelling, when history and tales of life were shared around hearths. But now that words were coded, no longer was it necessary for the teller of the tales to be present. This was the time when words became representations and silence was now not in the mind. Now written, words were a single shared experience between the author and the reader. Why would one read out loud in an empty room? Reading became a dialogue between two people, not a broadcast from one to many.

Each of us has our own silence. Mine is not the silence of space or the silence of a padded room. Mine is shared silence, a communal silence, a quietness. Perhaps John Cage's idea points me towards the notion of loss of awareness of sound. Listening to the sounds that lie within the frame of our existence reinforces the sense that we exist and that we are connected with that which makes us 'here'.

Christopher Isherwood: 'My will is to live according to my nature, and to find a place where I can be what I am.'

Two centuries ago, one was required to play an instrument or visit a concert for music. Then it was not possible to become tired of Bach's Cello Concerto in 'C'.

Today most sound is selfish and angry.

Except for me, in summer, at 1 Place de l'Eglise.

A Tale of a Tub

Chance encounter – Chelsea Henry – the confidence of the ignorant – a craftsman – transporting air – 600 all in.

12 July 2013

Dear Trevor,

Yes, I've got a bath! I bought it off a Frenchman I knew about twelve years ago, but never did anything with it. It has been sitting in the back garden of a house I used to live in in Chelsea. I'd almost forgotten I had it to be honest. I am looking for £600 – that is around the figure I paid. It has a certain rustic charm, as opposed to deluxe glamour. To be honest it is not as grand as some of the ones you see when you Google 'copper bath'. It hasn't got that curving lip all the way round, nor does it rise up at either end. It is flat topped.

But it has been in the garden for ten years so will need a polish. I'd be pleased to think of it being used and repatriated to France.

My friend who lives in my old house is away to Italy for a fortnight or so, but I can arrange to meet up one evening and show you when he gets back.

Best wishes
Andrew

In posh London between the King's Road and Chelsea Embankment there's a quiet, leafy square called Oakley Gardens. Around here the houses are as prim as a ladies' maid, except number 7, which is unusually scruffy. Unlike all the others in the street, you won't find flowers in pots around the front door, and there's a self-seeded buddleia in the small front garden. Someone has had a hack at it a while back, leaving a messy paroxysm of stems. Weeds grow on the short pathway of Peak Stone flags, now cracked and crumbling after 200 years of winter frosts. Decadent it certainly is. A little grimy, that's for sure. Though grimy in this road is kempt in any other.

One evening in early August, I met Andrew near the gate. He was casual and jolly, open-necked shirt and hail-fellow. The following year, he would appear in a documentary series called *The Auction House*, following the trials and tribulations of the staff at Lots Road Auctions. I seem to recall that all the male auctioneers looked exactly like Andrew. He knocked, and we passed the time of day as we waited. A minute went by, and he knocked again. After a scuffling and a clunk, the door drew inwards, dragging a small drift of junk mail across the floor, and there stood Henry.

'Ah, there you are,' he said as if we were late. 'Andrew, dear boy. What a delight. The bath. Come in, come in.' I couldn't see much of Henry at that moment, as the light was so dim, but as we walked the hallway into the kitchen, Henry was illuminated, revealing a Henry as Henrys should be, right down to the bow-tie, dishevelled three-piece tweed suit and pink nose. A glass of thick red grasped in his right hand sloshed as he offered his left hand, inverted, to shake. He was too slim for Uncle Monty, too tidy for Les Patterson, not spruce enough for Arthur Negus. He was a hotchpotch of them all. If he was famous, he would be just 'Henry', like Hoover, or Tupperware or Velcro.

'Come in, come in,' he repeated as he introduced himself. 'Henry. Lovely. Come in, come in.'

'Trevor. Nice to meet you.'

'A glass before business? I've got a nice red on the go.'

The red was at least halfway gone, but it stood on a table as a feature between two bowls of not quite identifiable nibbles and two glasses.

'Delighted, old boy,' said Andrew.

'Many thanks,' said I.

To the left of the small scullery kitchen was a very over-grown garden – overgrown as in 1950s bombsite. Vegetation was up to the windows with buddleia and rose bay willow herb tangled with bramble. We sat for a while, and Andrew and Henry caught up as I sipped what was in fact a really good bur-gundy. Then business turned to the bath, and we three trooped into the garden, which would only just about accommodate us as long as we tramped down some greenery. Just visible, in among it all, was the bath, black and bruised, one side of the base bumped, weeds growing in and around it. I fought my way over. It was also full of bricks.

'Don't quite remember how I got it here, or who I bought it from, or where precisely,' said Andrew going into auctioneer's mode as he watched my face drop. 'Though what I do know is that one like this done up would be worth thousands . . . if you could ever find one like this again – which I severely doubt. I seem to recall it came from northern France somewhere. If I dragged it out and took it down to Lots Road, I reckon it would go for double the six hundred pounds I'm asking. Bargain. The brass plughole is still here and although the iron foot and the iron around the top where the copper lips over is gone, and there are splits here and there and . . .' He stopped. 'Look, there it is. It's a bargain, old chap. Six hundred quid, and it's yours.'

'Great,' I said. 'If you drag it out, get rid of the bricks and make it tidy enough to get into a van, deal.' He smiled, and we shook hands.

'Two hundred quid, mate, door to door.'

'But it's as light as a feather and will take you an hour.'

'Volume, mate. It's the size, not the weight. If I put your bath in the van then it reduces what else I can carry.'

'I'll get back to you,' I said.

'Two hundred quid to transport it from Chelsea to here,' I shouted through to Kaz, who was doing . . . something . . . elsewhere.

'Jo's got a Volvo. I'll ask her,' she shouted back.

A week later, the bath was sitting in our living room on newspaper. We were walking round it as if we were in a small garage containing a large caravan.

'Shit, what have we done?' said I.

'Shit indeed. What indeed have *you* done? You said it would just need a bit of a polish.'

'Well, it does need a bit of a polish and a bit of an overhaul.'

Jo was now openly laughing her head off, having helped hoik it in through the front door from the car.

'And you can shut up.'

'It's lovely,' she said. 'It's unique. It's knackered, but it's lovely and unique.'

'Yes, but we need to make it lovely and unique and not knackered,' said Kaz, 'and it looks to me like an expensive business. How much did you say you bought it for?

'Four hundred quid.'

'Well, if we can bring this in for less than six hundred, I'll

III

be astonished and that's if we can find someone who can repair it for two hundred quid. This is a specialist job.'

'If we can bring it in for six hundred it will be a terrific buy. Do you know, if this had gone to auction, then it would have fetched at least double that?' We've got a bargain here. It's still got its brass plughole and everything.'

'Uniqueness and loveliness and everything!'

'Jo! Will you just shut the fuck up?' said Kaz.

'Sorry, yes. Have you got a tissue? I need to wipe my eyes.'

August turned to September, and September to October. And as the autumn leaves turned to the colour of our bath it remained stately in the middle of our living room, a feature for visitors, who encountered it with mixed reactions. Jo got used to it and was starting to take pride, like a foster parent might take pride in one of her charges who had managed to stay out of prison.

Kaz had been scouring the interweb for possible people who might restore it. Most backed off like we were offering stolen goods. Then she found another Andrew.

Dear Andrew,

We have an old bateau-style French copper bath that we want to restore as a workable bath. I have attached some photos to give a better idea of what's involved.

The bath is around a hundred and fifty years old and has spent the past ten years outside in a garden. It seems to be basically sound with no obvious leaks but as you will see from the photos it has some cracks around the top. The bottom plinth also needs straightening and strengthening – any steel or iron support it may originally have had is now completely missing and this needs replacing. The old solder along the seam between the base and side is also very rough. I assume it's lead and now quite brittle so this would also need removing and replacing. Apart from that it's in showroom condition.

As I explained, we would like it to be usable as a bath and so I think it needs professional cleaning, although we are keen to keep its character and patination – we don't want it to look new or highly polished.

I don't know whether this is the sort of project you ever take on but if so would you be able to give me some idea of the sort of cost and time involved. I also wonder if you are able to collect.

I look forward to hearing from you.

Regards
Kaz

Andrew was willing to take it on. But rather reluctantly, as he had promised himself he would never do another copper bath as 'they are such pigs'. Mrs D charmed him, but he couldn't start until the New Year and wouldn't pick up.

Christmas came and went, and on 3 January we hired a van from the Rent a Car at Lewisham and drove over to Andrew in Chertsey Road, Chobham. Leaving it in his hands with a friendly 'Nice bath. I'll be in touch. Bit busy but will get to it soonest.'

Then Chobham flooded.

It wasn't until April that we eventually got the call that the bath was ready for collection. In the meantime it had been bobbing around in the workshop among a whole flotilla of other floating objects. When the water went down, the bath was rescued, and work began. A new iron hoop had to be bent and slipped under the copper lip round the top. A new iron pad was made and copper strips soldered carefully – and obviously, since we wanted the new to show as new – over the splits. The bottom was made watertight, and the whole thing lightly cleaned. It took Andrew a month in total, on and off, to do it, and when we arrived to take it home it was a treat for the eyes. Our hobo of a bath was now spruced up and healthy, but still proud of its age. I'm not sure what it cost, but let's say, not including van hire, about two hundred quid, six hundred all in.

The next step was to get it down to the south of France. This was achieved by way of a man with a van who brought the cost from garden in Chelsea to sitting waiting to be installed in Languedoc at around, let me see, about six hundred quid. When François installed it, he had to put the drain under the floor, which meant taking half the kitchen ceiling out and putting in an inspection hatch so that if it leaked at any point in the future we would get to it. Now there it was, a year after Henry and Andrew, installed and ready to go.

Nothing cost us more than the bath. Six hundred quid is not a great deal for a tub tale like that, though. I've had two wallows in it so far, working out, *entre nous*, to five hundred quid each. Cheap at twice the price. As I soak, I imagine all the characters who will wallow in it after me and try not to think about the grimy bodies that have wallowed in it before me.

13

My Father's House

Selling 1 Place de l'Eglise – history – an unusual cave – the mystery of the Roman monuments – like father like son

Now and again, it crosses our minds to sell 1 Place de l'Eglise.

There's still too much work to do.

We can't afford it.

We need a pool – we really don't.

The village isn't what it used to be – it really is.

There are no shops.

The bar is terrible – not true.

We need a change.

There's a prettier village.

The roof leaks.

The *cave* is falling to pieces.

It's too cold in winter.

Then, on a warm spring evening, we sip cold Rosé de Bessan on the roof terrace listening to the peals of the Church of Our Lady of Purification, watching the kestrels shriek and circle the bell tower, the sky turning to blood as the sun sinks, Gramatik's 'Late Night Jazz' drifting from our neighbour's window at just the right volume, and we telepathically agree: 'What on earth were we thinking?'

There's something in the bones of 1 Place de l'Eglise that sings to us. Sometimes it echoes at night in the pitch dark, and I can see how a fever might bring to life imagined secrets from its thousand years. But I have never felt anything other than benevolence from its walls even when I'm on my own, and thunder is crashing and rain lashing. Do I believe in ghosts? Only ghosts of the mind. This is just as well, since 1 Place de l'Eglise is built on a Visigoth graveyard. When I occasionally mention this, it makes some people press their mouth with horror. But to my thinking it's just history. I like to think it's the good people who remain.

1 Place de l'Eglise is called the Château for no other reason than it is the biggest house in the inner *circulade* of the village surrounding the church. Nominally I suppose I'm the *seigneur* and Kaz is the *châtelaine* of Causses – though I'd like to see that one fly in the bar on a Saturday night. The archway into Place de l'Eglise dates from the same time as the house. The first record of it is in 1199 as the 'Castrum de Caucio'. A plaque on the Jules Milhau side says that it was owned by Raymond de Cabrières and Veziade d'Anduze, who gave alms to the Saint-Just cathedral in Narbonne, of 'three parts of the castle of Causses with all their belongings, the borie de Pradines and the wood of Mont Peyroux and the said terroir'. In the Middle Ages, the village was part of the Châtellenie of Cessenon, one of a network of small castles governed by bailiffs. In 1555, Jacques Guibert, Bailiff of Roque-brun, also became Bailiff of Causses, and the house stayed in his family until 1650. Bailiffs were hugely powerful, owning not just the land but pretty much everything that was in it, on it, or cultivated over it. They also elected officials, who in turn drew up the rules for tax collection and appointed the rural guards, effectively the police, and ran the 'justice system'. It was just about as feudal as you could get. The bailiffs were to all intents gods of their domain. By the start of the 1800s, Causses was owned by the lords of Murviel and was broken up and sold off in 1860.

The parish church of Causses, Église Notre-Dame de la Purification, was originally a chapel built in the tenth century

in the Romanesque style, with rounded arches on the windows and doors. A couple of hundred years later, in 1144, Abbot Suger began rebuilding parts of the Basilica of Saint-Denis north of Paris, combining new engineering and his belief that art was a way of serving and reaching God. He incorporated ribbed vaults and flying buttresses, which allowed for more delicate outer walls, large clerestory windows and, above all, in terms of its key recognition element, pointed arches. Originally called 'French Work' – *Opus Francigenum* – it was not christened 'Gothic' until three or four hundred years later.

The style was a sensation. By 1163, Notre-Dame in Paris was under construction, and eleven years later Canterbury Cathedral was being largely rebuilt in its current Gothic configuration, and many other cathedrals and churches were being erected across Europe.* It took another couple of hundred years to find its way to Causses' church, when a tower and two new chapels with Gothic ribbed vaults were added. On the outside, the Romanesque rounded doorway arch was replaced with a Gothic pointed arch and two pilasters on either side. It all looks very beautiful from our living-room window – though evidently not beautiful enough for some tourist in 1855, who decided it would benefit from further embellishment. So he carved into it his initials and the date.

The old ladies of the village look after the church. I see them often and I always say hello as they go in and out. I like to think they have a bit of a soft spot for me because I once did a John Robie on their behalf, climbed over a 35-foot-high gap from our terrace to next door's roof to rescue a cat . . . which then scratched me, and I nearly fell off. All the while, the old ladies were looking up from Place Jules Milhau shouting *'Mon dieu'*

* Ken Follett's novel *The Pillars of the Earth* is worth a read.

and 'Oo la la' (they really do say that) as I was putting my life on the line to rescue their moggy. Utterly exhausted, utterly petrified, I climbed down with the ungrateful animal. They thanked me as I staggered into the square and presented it to them. Then, on closer inspection, they decided it wasn't one of their cats after all, just a stray, and it would have got down on its own anyway. Nevertheless, I was Causses' celebrity cat catcher, *l'attrape-chat*, for at least a week.

The inside of the church is almost untouched from the time it was built, excluding the two small chapels and the tower. One of the bells dates from 1667 and it rather clanks when it's chimed, since it was cracked, so the story goes, when the bells were first rung after years of silence at 11 a.m. on 11 November 1918. The whole church was gently restored in the mid-1970s.

Just inside the archway entrance to the church square, our *cave* is on the left and next door's opposite – now bricked up – is on the right. Our *cave* was apparently where they kept the animals, including, it's said, the horses, and the other was for the guards. Our *cave* is unusual, as my walking companion had pointed out to me a few years before. More recently, I was loitering in the dining room, and a group of students entered the square. It turned out to be a class from Montpellier University looking at the medieval architecture. The professor pointed out the huge stones forming the lower levels of the outside wall of the house and then the different age layers as it was built up. There are four slit openings about 1.5 metres off the ground on the outside but inside about 3 metres up from the floor. I asked the leader of the group if she would like to look inside, and she jumped at the chance. My goodness, she was impressed. Very excited, she told me that the barrel roof was pretty standard but the fact that the curve of the roof came round one side and flared straight into the slit openings was very unusual. I got the impression that there were only a few that were like this in the area, the reason being they were quite difficult to construct and tended to fall down. She reassured me that since ours had been up for around 1,000 years it wasn't likely to collapse any time soon.

There is a wooden door in the corner of the *cave* leading into next door's stairwell, and they in turn have a door that leads to the next *cave* and so on all the way round what's left of the *circulade*. We've still got the original very ornate wine vats dating from the mid-1800s. Unusually, they are in perfect condition with all the plumbing and cast-iron covers and a marble top which could have come from the local – though long-shut-down – quarry a couple of miles away on the way to the village of St Nazare de Laderez. There are also four huge stone 'feet' which would have, by the look of the curve, cradled a barrel about 2.5 or 3 metres in diameter. When I've made a bob or two from you chaps having bought this book, then I'll get it all sorted out, and we can have a party in there. My dream is to turn it into a little theatre, the vats' top being the elevated stage and the knock-through into the other part of the house the backstage and dressing area, with the *cave* at the front providing room for an audience of about thirty to forty people.

Ancient history is not just in the village, it's all around. There's evidence of people living in or near Causses for 4,000 years. Iron Age funeral urns were dug up at Fonsalade, a couple of miles away over the fields in vineyards. But the most fascinating relics, in my view at any rate, are the two cylindrical stone pillars, about 6 metres high and 2.5 or 3 metres in diameter, in the fields as you approach the village from Murviel. There were lots of theories about how old they are and what they were used for, but in 2011 Roland Haurillon, an eminent French archaeologist, did a very simple thing to settle the argument. He asked the locals: 'Instead of imagining Roman trophy towers or an impractical wooden aqueduct, we should have listened to the old people of the village, who told us about the "source of the taps", "*pilas*" (in Occitan "stone basins") and the well-known local "lead field".'

All this added up to a simple explanation. The towers were part of an irrigation 'pipeline' from the village spring, which still exists on Rue de la Fontaine as Les Robinets (the taps), to the site of the lavish Roman villa at Veyran. The water flowed downhill via an underground lead pipe to the valley, creating pressure, then across the valley, the pressure being moderated by the towers, since the water had to rise up them into air basins on their tops using the inverted siphon system. I think it was done to stop what they call 'water hammer'. The lead has now gone, although it is still there in local folklore. During Haurillon's excavation, masonry pads were found every 3 metres or so under the soil on which the lead pipes were fixed, and 'elbows' on each side of the columns' foundations directed the pipe to the top. This wasn't a bespoke solution to the transport of water in Causses. It was a well-known piece of ancient engineering called a *souterazi* or *souterrain*, an underground passage or chamber. There are similar works at Pompeii and sites all over the old Roman Empire.

History in these parts is domestic. It's easy to see shadows of ordinary people living their lives. I often see ghosts toiling in the hot sun, waggons pulled by horses, their heads sagging under the weight of summer heat. I fancy I see scars on women's hands and sweat on their brows, hear the echo of hammering of stone and raised voices. In our *cave* there are men making wine, in the *grenier* they fork hay, faces covered against the dust. In bedrooms women sew, and in the window overlooking the church men smoke. Across the square Jules Milhau leaves for a council meeting, and a man creaks open the door of 1 Place de l'Eglise after a day in the fields. They mingle with my memories. Memories of family. Of George and Freya and Kaz. Memories of meals in the gathering twilight, morning walks before the heat sets in. Memories of George's raucous, all-consuming laughter, his face thrown back, utterly lost in the funny.

My father was always happiest in his garden on hot summer days, mithering amongst his vegetables. In his retirement he was always 'doing something down the garden'. As brown as a berry, whistling as he worked. We got to talking one evening as we watched a blood sun descend over his Derbyshire piece of earth. We were sipping cold white wine as he mused that his dream was to spend the rest of his days in the south of France, basking in the sunshine and the heat. He loved the heat. The hotter it got the more he purred. He could work in 30 degrees all day and come out smiling. 'One of these days,' I said, 'we'll buy somewhere down there.'

He phoned me on Tuesday in the third week of January 1999. He told me matter-of-factly that he had cancer, that it had spread to his liver, he had perhaps three months, no more. We had seen him only weeks before at Christmas. I said I would come immediately. He told me that it was OK, I was not to rush, he had time, he would expect me at the weekend. I said I was coming now. I put the phone down and told Kaz and the children, and the next morning we travelled up in the car: quiet, organized, sombre. When we arrived, my father was sitting in his usual chair, yellow from jaundice. He got up unsteadily, and I ushered him back to his seat. My mother was in the kitchen as she always was, preparing the evening meal, peeling potatoes, making shepherd's pie, boiling cabbage. I didn't kiss her hello. We didn't kiss much in our family.

We spent the day talking. This and that. What I was going

to do, how the children were, how Kaz was getting on. He was thin and coughed now and again, nothing dramatic. Only once did he let his guard down and say, 'I wish I could see how George and Freya turn out. I wonder what they will do and become.' I held back tears. We didn't cry much in our family.

That evening, we talked more without the TV on and in front of an open fire. I reminded him of the day a few years before when he had told me he had to have a heart bypass and that it would be eight months' wait on the National Health. We were sitting in the garden, enjoying the April warmth, watching the breeze brush the green barley in the next-door fields. I asked him if he had the money to go private. There was a long pause. Eventually he said yes but he would rather save it. 'How much is a summer worth?' I asked. There was another long pause. He got up and walked slowly to the house.

A week later, he phoned me at work. He said he'd booked himself into a private hospital. 'It's going to cost about £12,000, done by the end of May.' I was really pleased and said so. Would he like me to come up and take him to the hospital when he needed to? 'That would be very kind.'

I was, I think, around thirty-five years old when we got into the car and set off after breakfast for the hour drive. Unusually, he talked a good deal. I cannot remember about what. When we got there, I walked around and opened the door and picked up his bag. He took it from me. 'I'll take that, old man,' he said. 'I'll take it from here.' He shook my hand and walked away slowly across the car park.

Not late we went to bed. I didn't sleep much. I could hear him shuffling and my mother getting him water. He had moved into the third bedroom, the bedroom that had been my sister's. He didn't want to disturb my mother. She understood. He didn't come down that morning. The doctor came and prescribed morphine. I somehow knew that things were moving more quickly than was expected but I didn't register. I had to go home that evening so went in to see him. He hadn't wanted visitors during the day. He was propped up, slightly fallen to one side. He smiled as I came in. I said I had to go but would be back in the next few days. 'That's OK, old man,' he said slowly. 'I'm going nowhere.' I sat down next to him and said slowly, 'Thanks, Dad, thanks for everything. Sorry,' I said, 'that sounds like I'm thanking you for a roast dinner.' He chuckled and he hugged me, for the first time I could remember, he hugged me. I stood and walked to the door. I remember the boards creaking. I turned back to him, his eyes were closed.

He deteriorated fast, and I returned three days later when he was admitted to hospital. By then, he was not conscious. I spent his last night reading to him. My mother and sister had gone home to sleep, and I sat with him from around midnight. I had heard that it was hearing that went last, so I read to him. Periodically, I held his now thin and mottled hand. The sun came up around 6 a.m., and I watched the countryside around Ashbourne brighten. He died at 9 a.m. with a last great sigh.

Mid-afternoon, July, driving through the mountains to the Orb to swim. It is 38 degrees. I park the car, open the door, and a blast of hot air hits my face. The bitumen on the road is soft and scorching. I look up. Not far away an elderly man wearing a tattered, yellowing, wicker hat is stripped to the waist working his hillside vineyard. His skin is wrinkled, as brown as a berry. He stands, stretches his back and turns towards me.

14

Lunch with Cat and Bernard

Jules Milhau – tricks of the trade – Château d'Yquem –
Picpoul – 'Le Coin Perdu' – more than just stone

Causses-et-Veyran is almost dead centre of the wine Appel-
lation d'origine contrôlée (AOC) called St Chinian. It was
started in 1982 and enfolds the oldest wine-making area of the
Languedoc. Appropriate, because the great Jules Milhau was
born in Causses-et-Veyran. It's unlikely you've heard of him,
but he's one of the most famous Frenchmen of the twentieth
century. Through my window in the *grenier* I can see across his
eponymous square to his house upon which is a plaque: 'Ici
Naquit Jules Milhau 1903–1972 Maire de Causses-et-Veyran de
1945 à sa Mort'. He's buried in a big marble grave in Causses
cemetery 100 metres or so from here. I once saw a flickering
black-and-white home movie of Jules in his dotage walking
out of this house, locking the front door and proceeding past 1
Place de l'Eglise under the stone arch into the Place du Marché.
It was certainly Jules, but through the fuzz it might just as well
have been Pagnol's César Soubeyran, striding through Les Bas-
tides Blanches.

Jules grew up in Causses and went to school here, eventually studying maths and physics at Montpellier University
before going on to teach at the Lycée d'Agde on the coast along
from Béziers. Agde is now synonymous with the most famous
nudist beach in France – maybe even the world. In 1935, Jules
published a thesis entitled *Etude économétrique du prix du*

vin en France (*Economic Study of the Price of Wine in France*), in which he addressed a problem that had been a mess since forever, that of forecasting the wine price immediately the grapes were harvested, so creating a market for it. Jules did not just lay down the rules for the French wine economy but was also a great supporter of the mutualist movement and a political activist in Hérault, fighting for people's economic rights. His parents started one of the first mutual societies in France in Causses.

St Chinian has twenty villages as part of its AOC, with some really good vineyards within them. I'm not going to bang on about wine as I'll get into trouble. Particularly in France. Victor Hugo said, 'God made only water, but man made wine.' When it comes to wine there's no room for amateurs. I know this from personal experience.

Our neighbours Benkt and Neta – Swedish of course – are proper wine people. In fact, all the Swedes around our way are proper wine people. I asked them once why it was that Swedish people really knew a lot about good wine. In Sweden you can only buy takeaway alcohol from the 'Systembolaget' a state off-licence or liquor store. The price of alcohol is governed by the state through these places and is very high. About 50 per cent higher than nearby Germany for example. It's been like this for decades, and as a consequence two-thirds of Swedes are teetotal from Monday to Thursday. If you are a drinker, then the cost of good wine is not much more than rubbish wine, since the tax is so high. And that's why most reasonably affluent Swedes know about good wine.

My father was a wine merchant of sorts. In the early 1980s, he started supplying pubs and restaurants in the Derbyshire Dales. Apart from the tourist trade from Manchester and Sheffield, there was not much appetite down at the Combine and Cowpat for anything other than Black Tower and cider. But he persuaded a few of the more go-ahead restaurateurs and landlords to let him create a wine list on a profit-share basis. He managed the stock, keeping the list small, half familiar Liebfraumilch and the other half something a little more daring, Côtes du Rhône for example. It went well, built steadily, particularly in the restaurants. It didn't seem to cannibalize the traditional drink sales, as the wine was drunk with a meal, where previously they had just walked over from the bar. For himself he put together his own good little cellar – under the stairs – of Pomerol, Fronsac and Saint-Émilion, ticking the small vineyard bottles in his copy of Henri Enjalbert's *Great Bordeaux Wines*. I still have that book over on the shelf between his Clive Coates' *An Encyclopedia of the Wines and Domaines of France* and my John Timpson's *Country Churches*.

I knew absolutely nothing about wine at that time – not much more now – and truth be told wasn't much interested to find out. My dad thought that a shame. Once in a while he'd open a bottle of chateau-bottled Saint-Émilion and try and get me to do the 'sip, swill and swallow', all the while commentating on what I was supposed to be smelling and tasting.

I did eventually pick up a bit here and there, but my real education was a bit of an epiphany. Around 1999, I was invited to a meal at the Pont de la Tour at Butler's Wharf in London to mark the publication of a book. We had finished the main, when my Sort-of-Boss suggested to the famous Author that he choose a dessert wine. As the sommelier pitched up, I was keeping a weather eye and I could see much nodding and smiling. Then a second sommelier arrived, and I thought, 'Hello.' When I heard 'dessert wine', I was thinking a bottle of Muscat Beaumes de Venise or at a pinch a nice Hungarian Tokaji. But two sommeliers? Things were looking up. Maybe we are into Sauternes country here. The Sommelier Brothers reappeared with a trolley and a bottle, which looked like it had been in a bog for a hundred years, and proceeded to decant it. Little cut-glass glasses appeared round the table and I was getting all bouncy, nudging my neighbour, who was having a perfectly nice conversation. 'What?' came the tart response to the third nudge. 'Pay attention,' I said, 'I think the Author is about to bust the credit card.' He looked up as the little glasses were being filled with actual amber nectar. The Author didn't announce what he had just put in front of us, he just lifted his glass, sniffed, took the tiniest sip, closed his eyes and swallowed. So I did the same. I have never forgotten it. Sweeter than a first kiss. Sweeter than a choir of angels. Sweeter than a talced baby's bottom. More memorable than . . . I'm doing that wine thing aren't I? Seriously, though, it really was an epiphany. Not that anyone around me seemed to notice much. I lifted my glass to the Author as I caught his gaze, nodded my head just slightly and closed my eyes in reverence.

The next morning my voicemail red light was frantically blinking as I walked into the office. It was early. It was my Sort-of-Boss. I called her.

'Hello, it's Tre . . .'

'Did you know what the Author ordered last night?'

Me, bewildered. 'Well, I had the cod but . . .'

'What the hell! Do you know how much it cost?'

'Nothing to do with me. You told him to order the wine . . .'

The phone went dead.

Just to say, I asked the Sommelier Brothers what the wine was before I left. It was a 1983 Grand Cru Château d'Yquem. I asked if I could have the empty bottle. They said no and looked at me as if I were wearing a shell suit.*

When I first took Kaz to meet the parents, my father happened to be doing what all collectors of anything they collect do. He was counting his booty, wiping the dust off them, ticking them off in his book. They were laid out on the floor of his study. Sunday lunch came around, and he suggested to the future Mrs Dolby that she might choose a bottle from his little cellar. Off she went. I could see in my dad's eye the smug twinkle of 'Let's just see what she chooses, shall we?' Ten minutes went by, and back she came cradling a bottle which she timidly presented to my old man with the words, 'You said choose anything. Is this OK?' He took it, and his face slipped off as if the Ark of the Covenant had been opened in front of him. It was his prize bottle. His bluff had been called. The gunslinger had met Kaz the Kid. What could he do, other than say with stuttering bogus bravado: 'Great. Great choice.' God, I was proud.

But that wasn't good enough for my old man. Oh no. On subsequent visits my father and my future wife became like Withnail and Uncle Monty playing cards. Naturally I was Marwood. They pouted and they giggled as they chose a bottle, poured and sipped it, quoted unintelligible bons mots, toasted each other's sagacity. It was sickening. And *I* wasn't included. *I* wasn't allowed a glass. Pearls before swine. But then suddenly they started to include me. A glass of rusty red would appear with theirs. They asked my opinion. I glugged and said very

* Apparently it wasn't that I was an oik. Restaurants don't like giving out empty bottles when relieved of their expensive wine. They tend to end up on dodgy websites – shops in those days I guess – with a fresh cork, full of cheap plonk.

nice, and they giggled the more. It took me a while to figure out that they had been pouring me some old plonk while they had the good stuff. Funny. Bastards.

When we bought 1 Place de l'Eglise, Picpoul (some spell it Piquepoul, but they are wrong) was the club-footed local village-idiot wine bundled with cheap *formule* lunches. We loved it and would roam around looking for restaurants that included half a carafe in the price. We would trot off over to the village of Pinet and visit the *cave*, degustationing and stocking up for two or three euros a bottle.

The Picpoul area is a triangle between Agde, Pézenas and Sète, the hypotenuse running along the Etang de Thau.* By the by, Picpoul (pique-poul) means 'stings the lips' because it is high in acid, which is the reason it goes so well with seafood, cuts though the richness. It's also made from one grape, 'picpoul', making it easy to keep consistent.

Freya is the keeper of the oyster flame. It's hardly possible to distract Freya when she has an oyster in her hand. Straight from the freshly popped shell, slurped with a little vinegar and chopped shallots. 'You know they are alive?' I said once as we sat eating at a favourite restaurant overlooking the sea at Bouzigues. She looked at me quizzically and helped herself to another.

As time went on, Picpoul escaped and could be found in the odd local supermarket in Béziers. One day around 2008, I walked into a posh restaurant in London, and there it was on the menu. Thirty-five pounds a bottle.

* The Etang de Thau produces almost a tenth of all the oysters in France. Go to Les Jardins d'Oc at Bouzigues and order the *brasucade de moules*. My tip? Lick the outside of the shell after you've extracted the mussel. Honestly, you'll thank me.

There is actually a rosé Picpoul available from a few vineyards. It's not as acidic as the white, defeating Picpoul's *raison d'être* in my view. And then there is the mythical red that is used mainly for blending since it's high in alcohol and is very pale. All the locals we talked to about it said it wasn't particularly worth seeking out or drinking even if you could find it. That's why it was used for blending. But I wasn't buying that. I'd heard it was the good stuff. The last secret of Picpoul. I'd heard that some neat red could be had by those in the know, a tap of the nose, *j'ai du nez*. Then I met Bernard. It was my moment when Francis Duflot serves Max 'Le Coin Perdu'.

I have known Cat, a literary agent, on and off for about thirty years. She had bought a house near Carcassonne and was in the process of doing it up when we bought 1 Place de l'Eglise. In fact, I was on the phone to her when we had made the offer on the house in Magalas that fell though. She was on a bus from Carcassonne airport to her house. When she heard what we were up to, we kept in touch, and six or seven years later we eventually managed to arrange lunch.

It was just before midday when we arrived and were led to the terrace overlooking the vineyards and the mountains. The shade was from some sort of vine. Not like you see in Conran Shop adverts, not green and lush and trailing. This was proper. Browning, crisp in parts and unkempt, fallen leaves still lying on the old wooden table and ancient chipped floor tiles. Cat went to beaver away in the cool, dark kitchen.

And then Bernard appeared.

I'd known she had hooked up with a local, but there are locals and there is Bernard. He was covered in stone dust, cursorily shaven, thick set and sturdy, about sixty, though could have been fifty or seventy. He shook hands with me, kissed

Kaz three times left-right-left and enchantéd us. Cat returned. 'You'll have to make the most of him. He'll be off pretty much as soon as the meal's over. He gets up at five and works through to lunch at twelve. At precisely one o'clock, mid-sentence, he'll be off for his siesta.'

They first met apparently when Cat asked in the village if there was someone who could come and do some work for her on the house. Bernard had arrived one morning and never left. Cat couldn't speak much French at that time, and Bernard could speak absolutely no English. Match made in heaven.

Bernard had been to Montpellier once and didn't like it so had never been anywhere since. After he had been with Cat a few years, she bullied him to go to London with her, where she still has a house. He went and he didn't like that at all. It confirmed pretty much everything he had ever suspected about the human race. And the human race was welcome to itself.

Cat's house was done up as she earned the funds to pay for it. The roof one deal, the pool the next, until she had also bought the property next door 'to keep Bernard occupied'. To get into the new property, Bernard had bashed a hole in the ancient stone end-wall, making a door crafted to look as though it had been there for hundreds of years. The other side is a huge barn, a colossal barn. Bernard had already fixed the roof, but the underneath was like an Egyptian archaeological dig with ramps down to stone cellars. Large parts had been beautifully stone-masoned and pointed. It's so big there are internal pathways from one place to the next. Up old wooden staircases to a *grenier* the size of an aircraft hangar. Then down other stairs into another barn cleared down to the foundations. It was a marvel. Bernard had done everything. The stonework was perfect, the woodwork was perfect. The detail on the doors he had replaced would take a microscope to find fault with. It was a work of art. The thing with Bernard is he never does things to get them done. Time to Bernard is not something he is spending. It is something he is using. Something he is contributing to. Bernard does everything as well as possible, instead of as fast as possible.

Bernard still doesn't speak much English, but with my bit of French and Cat and Kaz's much better French the lunch progressed, and we laughed at the same things. Or I think we laughed at the same things. We ate a tomato tart, tomatoes grown by Bernard. '*Délicieux*,' I said. '*C'est rien*,' he said. Bernard told us about his allotment in the mountains, a piece of land he had cultivated for decades. Cat got rather testy, as he wouldn't tell her where it was, and she had never seen it.

At one o'clock Bernard got up as predicted and was off without a word. But to our surprise, about five minutes later, he returned with an unmarked green bottle with the cork out. Cat had eyes like saucers. 'Fucking hell, Dolby, what on earth have you been up to? Bernard never misses his siesta and absolutely NEVER shares his wine.' Bernard smiled. He knew pretty much every swear word. He poured, and out came a cool red wine. Not thick, not thin. Not deep red, but not pink. And cool, not from the fridge, but from a cellar cool. I sipped. Barnard leaned in.

'Picpoul,' he said conspiratorially.

'Eh?' I said in my best French.

'Picpoul,' he repeated.

Cat piped up. 'He's got Picpoul vines up at the allotment. He makes red Picpoul.'

'Get off with you. Really? Picpoul? Red?'

I don't know if it was the place and the person and the moment, but it was like being allowed to sneak a peek through the ajar door of a club whose members rule the world (otherwise known as the Beefsteak). As far as Bernard was concerned, no more was to be said. Here it was. It was his pleasure. Drink. Enjoy.

Bernard stayed on that afternoon and he took me on another slower tour of his handiwork. Then, around three, he decided that that was quite enough, nodded his head and slowly ambled away, his head down in thought, his right hand held high in valediction.

We left shortly after with a story and a gift from Bernard.

The gift of contentment.

15

A Blue Lizard and a Chanteuse

Death on the Orb – two roads diverge – an innkeeper – Jean-Paul Belmondo – love and kisses

One hot afternoon in June, I found myself drowning in the River Orb. I'd been swimming with a capybara* under the medieval bridge when I ran the rapids at the mill. This was when France was still a place where it was your own fault if you were stupid enough to injure or kill yourself. Our Anglo-Saxon attitude toward risk was not, fifteen years ago, that of our Gallic chums. Unlike the UK, where there were signs on just about everything telling us that it will kill us, in France your stupidity was your own affair. Want to smoke yourself to death? *Fumez tout le jour, mon frère.* Drink until your liver is pickled? *Santé, copain!* Watch someone overtake you on a blind bend and get hit by a lorry? Your fault, because you were going too slow. Electricity pylons tell the tale.

In the English countryside they are barbed-wire-fenced and mini-minefielded, topped with huge signs sporting stick men poleaxed by a lightning bolt. Underneath are the words 'DANGER OF DEATH! Don't climb this. And if you do,

---

* There really was a lovely big capybara living on the river at Roquebrun. Big, healthy chap he was. Head like a carthorse, behind like a gigantic guinea pig. He'd mind his own business swimming up and down near the bridge. The locals didn't turn a hair. Now and again, tourists would notice: 'Look! Look! There's a pony in the river!'

when you get up there don't swing from the wire. It will kill you.' In France? Nothing. In the mountains, if you want to shin up a pylon and do your best Philippe Petit, then that's your issue. *Tant pis.*

Driving the mountain road to Le Lézard Bleu restaurant is a personal case in point. I've done it hundreds of times. It's just about wide enough for one car. Life lesson in France: in these situations it's the car width of the car heading towards you that the road is one car wide for, and not yours. I had a parallel-universe moment on the way to Vieussan. For 5 kilometres or so there is just rock on the right and a 100-metre drop on the left, except for one 50-metre passing place about halfway along. We were run off the road at exactly that passing point. Any other place we would have been *entrecôte*. I cross myself and Hail Mary when we pass it now. It seems polite to thank something.

So there I was, swimming along with Roquebrun on the left, my friend the capybara having paddled in the other direction. It really is chocolate-box lovely is Roquebrun. The stone houses hugging the hillside, the village topped by a medieval tower and Mediterranean garden. In front of me there is a weir directing water along the side in a nice gentle tinkle. To the right is a sluice with a Hoover Dam torrent of water pouring through it like liquid lead. As I get closer, I can feel the pull of the current through the sluice. I look around. No signs, no warning. OK, I think, no danger, and carry on as the current starts to tug on me. Then things get hairy. I am suddenly gripped by a huge hand as the water gets thicker and thicker and drags me faster and faster towards the sluice. I think I'm a pretty level-headed sort of chap, but believe me I'm panicking. I can see the water in a great mellifluous surge going through the gate at a rate of knots followed by a drop of over a metre into a roaring torrent. I'm really moving now and as the sluice comes toward me I grab at anything I can. Bingo. A bar on the side, obviously where the gates were once hinged. This is where you picture Buster Keaton in a hurricane, horizontal, holding his hat on with one hand, the other on a door handle. This isn't going to end well. I am quickly ripped from the bar and tossed under water into the boiling mess. In the tumble all I can think of is to protect my head, so I wrap my arms around it as best I can and then over I go. You know what I thought as I headed to oblivion? 'I should have taken my glasses off.' Yup, what sort of idiot wears glasses when he's swimming. Bump . . . I hit something on my left, a broken arm. Crunch . . . a smashed knee. Bang . . . the hand over my head hits a rock. I am starting to feel really woozy.

Of course I survive, the thrill here is in what condition. I pop to the surface, grab a rock, slither up the side to face my aghast audience, who have seen the whole thing unfold. I look up, and nothing. No one, it seems, not one of the 200 people in or around have even noticed. I inspect my damage. Blood all over the arm, leg and hand. But intact. I stagger to the shore. An English voice chirrups up. 'Hellah. Are you a k? Saw you gay aver the wear. Mad. Nay warnin sign. People'll get killed gaying aver thar. You a k?'

That evening, we decided dinner at Le Lézard Bleu was required to celebrate my reprieve. Roquebrun is about a third of the way to Vieussan from Causses, passing though a village called Ceps, then making a steep climb up into the mountains. We try to leave it as late as possible, as the sunsets up there are sublime. I drive. Mrs Dolby is not one for jousting with Citroëns on mountain roads.

KAZ: You going to take off my glasses before we go into the restaurant? I can't believe you only brought one pair down.

ME: Why? I won't be able to see the menu.

KAZ: You look like Dame Edna Everage.

ME: I thought I might pass as Audrey Hepburn in *Breakfast at Tiffany's*. You know, the bit when Rusty Trawler arrives at the party. I want a name like Rusty Trawler. How about Brick Layer?

KAZ: Audrey Hepburn didn't wear glasses in any of her films. She wore sunglasses. Cat's-eye sunglasses.

ME: Yes, like these.

KAZ: You look about as much like Audrey Hepburn as I look like Winston Churchill . . . *Don't even think about it!*

ME: Good job our prescriptions are similar.

KAZ: Similar but reversed.

ME: That's why I'm wearing them upside down.

KAZ: I was wondering why you had elastic bands round the back of your head.

ME: That's nothing to do with the glasses – they're holding my skull on. Apart from the broken arm, the broken leg and the broken hand I also have a piece of my skull missing.

KAZ: That was awful, but don't be a drama queen. Your skull is fine.

ME: Thanks. Nice to hear some concern.

KAZ: I was really concerned. You frightened me to death. Seeing you staggering toward us with blood all over you. I was nearly hysterical.

All that flashed through my mind was: who
would I find not to do the ironing? Not to cook?
Not to take out the bins?

We first stumbled across Le Lézard Bleu not long after our
first summer. I have to be careful here. Claiming discovery
rights on Le Lézard is dangerous. It's divorce territory. The
truth is that Kaz and George and Freya found it when I was
back in London and they were looking for a place to swim on
the Orb, away from the crowds at Roquebrun and before we
had been let into the secret location of Causses beach. I might
tell you in book two. They had been swimming at the river in
Vieussan when they decided they needed an afternoon drink,
and as they turned right off the bridge, there was Le Lézard
Bleu like an apparition. It's just about unique in and around
the area now where once Lézard-like was the norm. Now there
are more pizza places in Languedoc than in Italy. Le Lézard is
like going back in time.

When we holidayed in Provence in the early 1990s, we had
lunch at the Café de la Gare at Bonnieux, then still much like
Peter Mayle had described in his book *A Year in Provence* of
three or four years before. I seem to remember an unmarked
door in an old house next to the disused railway station along
a dusty, rutted track. At precisely midday, tractors and old
Renault 4s would arrive almost in convoy. Old young men
in dirty dungarees and old old men straight out of *Jean de
Florette* ambled in. Having been tipped off, we arrived and tentatively tested the door. We couldn't get in. The door handle,
we quickly learned, opened the opposite way. Inside, it was
smoke-filled and smelled a little like the rhino house at London
Zoo. Every head in the place, all male, turned as one as if we
had dismounted ashen horses. There was no menu. Périgord

tumblers were tossed onto the table and an unmarked bottle filled with what looked like watery red wine. A napkin full of torn baguette arrived, and then immediately after plates of what looked like chicken stew. It was hard to tell, as the place was as dark as the inside of an old man's lung. There was no sound other than that of forks and knives hitting plates. In we dived. It was just divine. Thick and meaty, dense and treacly. We followed our neighbours, plunging lumps of fluffy, crisp white bread into the broth, pushing it into our mouths. The wine was indeed watery but just perfect to throw down after the bread and broth. I doubt there was much alcohol in it. It was perfectly thin. Made for the job. Like small beer.

It took all of fifteen minutes to finish and be on our way. I cannot remember what it cost. Probably 40 francs (£4) a head, maybe less. We talked about that meal for years before we managed to get back. By then, Mayle mania had arrived, and the place had been sold and had a reception desk, menus, table-cloths and sunlight. There was a table-tennis table on a new-laid lawn at the rear. Eventually Pierre Cardin bought it and put framed black-and-white photos on the walls.

Across the gorge bridge then down the valley, the village of Vieussan is on the right, clinging to the mountainside like scree. At the bottom, by the river, is Le Lézard Bleu.

We had been going to Le Lézard for ten years before we got to know Rik Kat. Every time we went, I would book in my pidgin French – a table on the terrace. We would turn up and be greeted in French. We would order in French – 'Le Menu' – we would eat, thank him, pay and leave. Over the years we realized Rik could speak perfect English, German, French and Dutch. But we had made our bed. When we went to Le Lézard in winter, we were just about the only people in there apart from the locals who drank and laughed in the bar.

Rik set a table for us next to a huge log-burning stove, black with soot, drifts of grey ash under the grate. It was warm and snug as the cold wind tumbled down the valley past the clattering windows and we sipped syrupy red St Chinian wine and tucked into pork stew and potatoes. I got to know Rik's collection of lagers. There must be about 100 different brands stacked behind the bar and in a tall fridge next to the toilets. The toilets are a feature. The mascot of Le Lézard is a blue cartoon lizard that instructs the clientele as to their micturating responsibilities.

One cold evening, we broke the ice. On the walls are artworks from classic album covers: *The Court of the Crimson King*, *Led Zep IV*, Bowie's *Pin Ups*. Artworks, not the covers themselves. Copies, of course. A terrific collection. The best of the best. We got talking in English, and goodness, he knows his stuff. The story goes, and I've not verified it with Rik because it's too good to be wrong, that he arrived in the south of France in the 1980s on a mission from Holland to meet some of his mates at Roquebrune for the summer. Rik duly pitched up at Roquebrun. Roquebrune (Cap-Martin), where his chums were partying, is between Monaco and Menton, pretty much on the Italian border, about 500 kilometres away. On reaching Roquebrun, he decided it was too much of a drag to go all the way over to Roquebrune and stayed, met his wife, Manue, and eventually started Le Lézard Bleu in an old coach house which had been serving customers since the 1850s. Over decades it had gone out of business, back in business, out of business, back in business. The Kats had been there perhaps fifteen or so years before we arrived, Manue in the kitchen, Rik out front.

If you look on Tripadvisor – quite why you'd want to is beyond me, but people do – you'll find pretty much all the reviews are 'Excellent' or 'Very Good'. There are two or three marked 'Poor' that say much more about the people who write them than about Le Lézard: along the lines of 'We turned up with a party of 300 and they couldn't fit us in. I was aghast. Don't these peasants want our business?'

As we got to know Rik it was apparent he knew all about us. How were our children? How was Causses? What's London like these days? I laughed: why hadn't he spoken before? He shrugged, 'You seem to want to do your thing, try out your French, have your meal and go.' He shrugged again. 'I'm an innkeeper.'

The terrace at Le Lézard is my happy place. I can close my eyes and feel the warm summer breeze on my face rustling the overhanging lime tree, the coloured lights coming on in the late evening, the bustle of greetings, the hubbub of languages, supper cooked like at home, but you wouldn't cook at home.

Then into the car for the slow drive back as the heat of the day leaks into the sky and the darkness settles softly onto the mountains and into the valleys. Most nights it's a quiet drive. But one evening, a genet stood in the middle of the road as the headlights reflected into its pink eyes, its long striped tail and spotted body thick and healthy. It wasn't concerned. It looked at us and ambled off into the garrigue. Not much further on, we had to stop again and watch a family of *sangliers* – wild boar – amble across the road, sow at the front, a line of boarlets and then the old man patrolling the rear.

If Le Lézard is like the Angler's Rest, then the bar in Causses is like the Queen Vic. Everything is drama at Causses bar.

After Dido left, it remained empty for a while, but soon René and Patricia arrived. René was straight out of central casting, a rural Jean-Paul Belmondo. It wasn't a stretch to see him on the run with Jean Seberg. When he and Patricia arrived a few years back, he was in his early sixties, warm and kind, thoughtful and silent. They had owned a seafood shop and restaurant near the coast at Mèze and had wanted a change of life, so they moved to Causses, where they continued to serve the most delicious tapas: garlic prawns, *couteau* (razor clams), *tourteau* (crab), oysters from Bouzigues. René was taciturn but just oozed charm and calm.

He would open the bar at 7 a.m. and sit outside smoking cigarettes that smelled of tar, drinking coffee that looked like tar. He had a second sense about people. As you finished your glass of rosé, he could tell if you were staying or going. As the glass hit the table, he would fill it up in such a way as you hardly noticed.

René does not speak English. At all. It is not his plan to speak English. Ever. Language is just too divisive for René. Who cares? People are who they are to René. Being around him made people content. Not that he didn't have an opinion. His view was shown by a look there and sigh here. In a world where gossip is currency, René was the poorest in the village, but richer than them all.

And then there was Patricia. As René was tall and slim, Patricia was curvy and small. Where René was quiet, Patricia was as fired as Katherine of Padua. And she could drink. And it was all René's fault that she drank. René, and the bar, which she loved, because she loved people, but hated, because of the hours she spent there. René. Her husband. The most beautiful man she had ever seen, who had now lost his passion.

Patricia shared her sadness in the only way she knew how. She sang. My goodness, she sang. A few drinks, and past midnight she would rise unsteadily and unbidden and sing Edith Piaf better than Edith Piaf. A cappella. Eyes closed, hands to the sky, then tumbling down as if strings to her head had been snipped, falling in despair as the words demanded. She had the heart and soul and talent of a chanteuse. But the world had conspired to ignore it. Her songs would be directed at René, who protected himself with clouds of smoke. And after, she would call him a heartless fool and lament his insouciance and she would drop weeping and angry on our shoulders, and we would console her, until suddenly she would fight free, at once cold and sober, turn to René and shout '*Mon amour*' and throw herself on him, showering him with sweet, drunken kisses.

16

One Better Day

*We'll walk there as the sun goes down – the rent was low, the
smell was rancid – a dysfunctional family – books*

1978. How lucky I was.

I had graduated with a poor degree in a poor subject from
a poor polytechnic. I had scarpered from the boondocks and
through much good fortune met a girl with a foundling mind
who took a chance. She gave me a job in London's Camden
Lock at a time when it was alive with talent and promise.

Today, pubs and restaurants in Camden are chic canteens
for the transitory famous who live just a Bafta's throw away
in Primrose Hill. Then, bars were gravy-coloured, mahogany-
panelled refuges from the grey streets of north London. The
Hawley Arms became my local in the month Sid killed Nancy.
A Victorian knees-up of a pub, stark and cold, the bar top
rugged with sticky, pale-ale-soaked towels, accessorized with a
plastic pineapple ice-bucket, a gallon jar of grey pickled eggs
and Marston's Pedigree, Theakston's, Young's, Watney's, Double
Diamond, Worthington's and warm Guinness. The ashtrays
demonstrated the Hawley had commitment, stacked, as they
always were, to overflow with the ash and ends of B & H,
Number 6 and Marlboro. Behind the bar was a mouldy mess
of old wooden cutting boards for wizened lemons, rubbed
and coppering silver-plate $\frac{1}{6}$ of a gill measures, stale drying-
up cloths, an unused stainless-steel sink, below optics of thin
gin, cheap whisky and too-sweet vermouth. The room was a

cave lined with Lincrusta, ill with cigarette tar, hung with a few grubby pound prints of ruined abbeys. Written in the thick nicotine dirt of Fountains was the plea 'fuckin clean me'. For the few years I drank there, no one ever did.

I worked over the road at a small publisher of illustrated books in Commercial Place, up a pine staircase to a loft overlooking the narrow-boat lock and the entrance to the then famous music venue T. E. Dingwall. New Leaf Books was under the eaves.

Everywhere was red pine and the smell of unseasoned wood and of glue. The floor was covered in jute matting, the desks aligned in two rented ranks. Those over five feet six tall were obliged to duck below the roof beams, and the windows rattled when the wind got up. Everyone's companion was Jake, an Old English Sheepdog who spent his days wriggling on his back, waiting for a tummy tickle.

In 1980, the old Gilbey's bottle store warehouse next to the Lock burned down in a national-newsworthy conflagration that took our wooden staircase with it. For a while we entered via an aluminium ladder. In the winter, the pipes froze, and we pissed in Dingwall's toilets. Between there and the office we sometimes hung out with eager unknowns like The Police.

The Lock was in much demand by film companies, and often we would sneak into their catering queue. One day, I stood in line with David Niven and Burt Reynolds, on another I passed the time of day with Suggs.

On the right, second desk in, was Michael McGuinness, an aloof, it seemed to me, illustrator who, with steel-nibbed dipping pens, was illustrating a book which became the classic *Einstein for Beginners*. It was he who told me to listen to a new radio programme called *The Hitchhiker's Guide to the Galaxy*, just airing on the BBC. He had, he said, gone to the recording at the Paris Studios on Lower Regent Street. Just one of the ten or twenty thousand people who were in the 400-odd-seat theatre at the time.

In front of him was a picture researcher, Jackum, owner of Jake the dog. Jackum wore a peacock-feather cloak and refused to walk on the jute floor in case it 'earthed her spirit'. She leaped from desk to desk, scattering belongings without sanction. Some mornings she would leave a gift of dope, wrapped toffee-like in silver paper, on my S3GN Olympia typewriter. The actress Eileen Way was her aunt. I met her on the stairs one day and wanted to tell her *The Vikings* was a favourite movie, 'Ohhhdin, Ohhhdin, send the waves and turn the tide,' I recited, but just to myself.

Opposite was Celia, a red-haired book designer: punctilious, eager to make me feel at home. Her partner was Alan Gowan, keyboard for, at various moments, the Canterbury bands Gilgamesh, Soft Heap and National Health with Dave Stewart and Hugh Hopper. Sally, her best friend and my boss, had a thing for him. When he died of leukaemia in 1981, she and Sally cried together at his benefit at the 100 Club, where they played his epitaph to himself, 'Before a Word Is Said', and Celia's favourite, 'Fishtank', written by Alan and Hugh Hopper from their album *Two Rainbows Daily*. One cold Wednesday December morning in 1980, I was in early and found Celia already there. She told me that John Lennon was dead.

Further down on the right was Marilyn, who designed and created packaging artwork for everything from seeds to cosmetics. Thin and bohemian, smiley and warm, she rolled Golden Virginia into perfect cigarettes with her left hand while painting delicate watercolours with her right. I used to visit her flat in Hillgrove Road, West Hampstead, which she shared with her partner Ken Ansell, he who was to design the sleeve to The Human League's *Dare*, the Virgin logo and much else.

Much else included designing a book called *Rock Stars in Their Underpants* for Paula Yates. A year younger than me exactly, she had posed nude and taken up with Bob Geldof, then a mouthy singer in a middling band called the Boomtown Rats. She visited the loft one day: red lips and peroxide hair, so confident, so out there. Two years later, she opened on *The Tube* with an unknown keyboard player from Squeeze.

On the left, taking up two desks, was, periodically, Terry Jones, the legendary editor of Italian *Vogue*. He was creating *ID* magazine, the first edition of which was published in 1980. His coterie of hip young assistants unnerved me with their skinny confidence and T-shirt-tensioning nipples. Had I been a different person, I might have bumped into Dylan Jones and been invited to Billy's and Blitz.

The owner of the company sat farthest from the ply door, facing out towards the canal through a four-pane window, his back to a large meeting table. He turned forty the second year I was there. I was never sure of him. He was, I thought, not a little Widmerpool-ish. He was a talented editor and had his own small publishing company. No mean achievement, it seemed to me, at the time of my life when everything seemed possible.

Sally had interviewed me for researcher and liked my college project, which looked at fungal infection in beet-seed viability. I said if she liked it enough she could have the rights to publish it. A bad joke she saw through as nervousness and offered me the job.

They all instantly became my family. Mad and self-obsessed, generous and confused.

*

For those who worked there, Camden Lock was a market where the most valuable commodity was self-esteem gained by one's skill in making and creating 'things' and by the cultivation of a character that exhibited well. I was an absolute beginner, a lad of meagre ambition travelling from a sour, settle-for Midland town. I had been sullen and bemused at college but in London I came alive, blood pumped by Joe Strummer and Paul Weller and *All Mod Cons*.

On the right, under the railway bridge and over the canal, was Zipper, a gay bookshop that was raided by the police so regularly that it became a spectator sport. The rozzers pitched up once a month in vans big enough to take their entire stock of dodgy mags. The word went round, and we all trooped out to shout and jeer.

On the left, almost opposite Zipper, at 234, was Anne Shepherd, Diana Gravill and Nicholas Rochford's Compendium Bookshop, then just ten or eleven years old and regarded as the finest, most radical bookshop in Britain. We locals got to know it as a glum place that believed the world didn't deserve them.

On the corner of Jamestown Road I always seemed to be running into an androgynous young man who wore extravagant make-up – slightly unusual but nothing to write home about. Then he was Stuart Goddard; later he was Adam Ant.

In Arlington Road was the red-brick monolith that was Arlington House, former home of, among many lost lives, Brendan Behan. It was the biggest doss house in north London, opened in 1905 by the Victorian philanthropist Lord Rowton. Orwell stayed there, and his description in *Down and Out in Paris and London* makes it sound a strangely edifying place:

> The best [lodging houses] are the Rowton Houses, where the charge is a shilling, for which you get a cubicle to

yourself, and the use of excellent bathrooms. You can also pay half a crown for a special, which is practically hotel accommodation. The Rowton Houses are splendid buildings, and the only objection to them is the strict discipline, with rules against cooking, card playing, etc.

By 1978, the building was ragworted and mossed, paint-flaked and gone, brickwork no longer red but black and cracked and failing. Forty-five years after Orwell, the regime was unchanged; by then it seemed harsh, uncompromising, uncompassionate and unnecessarily disciplinary. Every day, hundreds of homeless, mostly alcoholics – though known then as 'drunks', as pejorative and flippant a word for their condition as there could be – were turfed out, as costers set up in Inverness Street next door, to scrounge money to buy cider to make the day go away.

Now Arlington House is home to the Museum of Happiness.

Each morning, on my walk from Camden tube I would pass the same battered, dirty, scabbed faces looking for their first drink. This was long before Class A was peddled openly, although I was always being offered 'lucky bags', an unspecified selection of five or ten different uppers or downers. Alcohol was, and is, just as wicked, perhaps even more so. One man who I knew as John could be found halfway up the high street, rhythmically banging his head on the wire protector around a young tree. Often I would say, 'Hello' or ask 'You OK?' or 'Can I help?' But for him I was not there, and he carried on until the scabs on his forehead opened and bled and then he moved on to his next routine of the day.

As autumn turned to winter, each week I would be given designers' instructions to acquire reference material for illustrators to create detailed artwork for the books we were working on. One week it would be for the cross-section of a cat's skin, or the migration route of the Arctic tern, the next the precise colour of civet fur or the lifecycle of a nematode worm. I would travel to libraries over London, photocopying and making notes and making up briefing packs that I then delivered a few days later, talking designers through and making sketches and notes for the illustrators. At the same meeting I would look at last week's batch of roughs made from the previous week's references, giving my thoughts and making amendments. Soon, I was asked to write captions and then articles.

I had no idea at the time how lucky I was. Everything here was helter-skelter, fast and furious, exciting and loud. Here, I was with talented people who made me think maybe I was talented too.

I was the age when noise is the thing most in demand. The crash of tube trains, the roar of traffic, the world shouting and chasing. I was grateful and proud to be included in the rush. Noise said I am busy, I am a part of things, one of an eager, vast and untutored cohort commanded by the need to belong. Once I queued for hours to get into the Camden Palais, the place to be seen, part of Steve Strange and Rusty Egan's demesne. But there was no entry for spectators like me. Much later, I knew Steve Strange, his life still orbiting, looking for ways to make his good times come again.

I lived in a flat above a butcher's shop in Kensal Rise. The smell was rancid, the rent was low. Our Greek landlord left us to ourselves, and we paid in cash. There were three of us to start, and girlfriends came and went, until after a year or two my friends left, one to return home to the quiet of rural Staffordshire – he wasn't cut out, he said, for London – and the other for a lucrative corporate life. I was on my own in this big place: four cold granny bedrooms, a living room from Rattigan's *Deep Blue Sea*, a kitchen from *Withnail and I*, dirty, stark and frayed.

I had come alive and wanted to fill every moment. I sat in front of a black-and-white TV or a Bush radio and read books. I didn't watch or listen much, I needed background chatter. It seemed to allow me to concentrate more on the words and allow the author to create our noise. Somehow I had found an intensity, and I read a book a day. I picked American literature and worked my way through Carson McCullers, Faulkner, Salinger, Hemingway, John Dos Passos, Sherwood Anderson, Steinbeck and Updike, William Styron, Gore Vidal and all the rest. I read hard among my own hubbub. And chink by chink, in the evenings, at weekends, walking up the stairs from the street, sitting in the corner of the Hawley Arms, in the pauses between sips or buses' rumble, I found something to love.

Forty years later, I sit reading Anthony Powell's *At Lady Molly's* in the spring sunshine at 1 Place de l'Eglise. A decade before, I had bought at auction Sir David Piper's complete set of *Dance to the Music of Time* for the handsome sum of £120: six first editions and sundries, with wonderful dust jackets illustrated by the then glitteringly famous Osbert Lancaster. It was a cold winter afternoon when I got them home. I opened *Books Do Furnish a Room*, enjoying the musty smell of maturing paper, turning each page with the same satisfaction and anticipation that Piper must have experienced forty years before. I placed it down, picked up the copy of *Hearing Secret Harmonies*, and out dropped two letters.

Dear David,

I was very grateful for your sending the copy of your note about the supposed Aubrey miniature, which I had a look at last Tuesday at Christie's. My own feeling is that it does represent Aubrey (and I have written to John Kerslake expressing that view), but I do, of course, see that it is open to objection. It may be that hauling the miniature out of its closely built-in frame might reveal something.

With any luck I shall finish the last vol by Christmas. If that comes off, it should be out by late summer. It is to be called 'Hearing Secret Harmonies'. You made a remark in your review of its predecessor, which showed almost telepathic prescience, and was already true at the time of writing it. I will not say what it was, but when vol 12 appears I think it will amuse you.

Yours,
Tony

Dear Tony,

Thank you for your letter with which, of course, I disagree.

Startled by your last paragraph, which is flattering but, I trust, not merely an ingenious device to make sure of a sale of at any rate one copy. Anyway I await the outcome with interest.

I liked your Maurice Bowra contribution very much. Isaiah Berlin was at dinner last night coruscating on it.

Yours sincerely,
David Piper
Director

I look to the right into the *grenier*, where I have a small library of books I love. I turn them face out as I remove and replace them, a revolving art gallery of new and old friends. I am constantly aware of the crowd of characters around me talking and moving, constantly living out vivid lives in the past, the present and the future. My books are a personal cacophony of places and people. I sit among them and as I glance up they go on their way as the writer intended, but I add to them my story: where I read them, who I was with, who I was at that time. These books are largely what I am.

I have a Yale edition of Boswell's *London Journal* – I've just taken it down from its shelf. I don't have to open it. Inside I know the old rogue is there, angsting over his worth and his talent. I also know that it is the book I read to my father the night he died. I rest my hand on it and I'm closer to him.

In unfamiliar homes I hunt down bookshelves, Billy or bespoke. I look for hints of who the owner is: what they think, their aspirations, their personality, their beliefs and prejudices, their passions and predilections. A collection of books is as unique and telling as lines on a face. Without books on paper how would great men show off their wealth in money and conceit? How would we impress a new friend? How could I lend my beautiful first edition of A. Scott Berg's *Max Perkins: An Editor of Genius* to a fellow who admired it; perhaps a new friendship made? Why do we feel it is a sin to throw away books no matter that they are tattered Penguins? Who could argue that a day spent on Ed Maggs' website is as fulfilling as a day among his shelves?

I remember the journalist Hugh Sykes broadcasting many years ago about a visit Michael Morpurgo made to east Jerusalem, promoting his then new book *Shadow*. He mentioned Hind Kabawat, a Syrian lawyer who specializes in conflict resolution. 'In her fabulous, spacious, stone Damascus house – with a fountain in the courtyard and elaborately painted high ceilings – she proudly pointed to the most important books on her shelf: the Bible, the Koran and The Sayings of Mahatma Gandhi.'

Facebook founder Mark Zuckerberg announced some years ago a new online messaging program to replace 'long-winded email'. He suggested with alacrity: 'communication 2.0 must be seamless, informal, immediate, personal, simple, minimal, and short'. An alarmingly powerful, ignorant young man with no sense of what enriches his fellow human's feeling of self, and self-worth. Today we have Twitter.

I go back to my book knowing that I have more memories now than memories I will make. I am a far cry from Camden.

17

The Secret of Fig Jam

Figs – festivals – la vendange *– the Thompson
Twins – poo bags and purple gold –
cross-examination – jam today*

We are at dinner with Hans and Lotten. They produce the most delicious, plump, soft, black figs.

'Wow, where did you get these?'

'It's a little secret'.

'What do you mean it's a secret? We're your friends. Did you buy them? Did you pick them?'

'We picked them off the fig tree this morning.'

'What fig tree?'

'*The* fig tree. The best fig tree in the village.'

'There's a best fig tree in the village? Who knew?'

'Well, everyone knows.'

'I don't know. Where is it?'

Hans and Lotten look at each other sheepishly.

'We'll have to see if we can tell you. We have some fig jam from last year from the same source, if you would like to try.' She goes over to a cupboard

'It needs a meeting?'

'Well, sort of.'

'What is this fig tree? The Singing Ringing Tree? The tree with the Golden Fleece?'

'That's an apple tree,' says Kaz.

I shoot her a glance that shouts smartarse.

'What's the Singing Ringing Tree?' says Lotten.

Kaz ignores me. 'These figs are really good, can we take a couple?'

'Try the jam,' says Lotten.

I try it, and it's the sort of jam I wanted to bury my face in and rub all over Mrs Dolby.

'Of course,' says Hans, 'would you like some cheese?'

'Cheese!' I cry, jam all round my mouth. 'Cheese?'

Wild food is a big thing in rural France. There is huge prestige in knowing the best places to dig stuff up, pick stuff or kill stuff. To know where the best mushrooms are, the best berries, the best fishing place, the best hunting place, the best olive trees . . . the best fig trees conveys real status. If you know these things then you, my friend, you are a don of the terroir, a gastronomic god. And the rule to rule all rules is *omertà*. The way to remain a gastronomic god is to keep things to yourself: 'here hare here'.

The snaffling starts in the spring, when the sky turns a fresh neon-blue and the sun begins to shine and the vines are spruce and smart from their winter coiffure. From November to March the *vignerons* have been pruning. Until recently, it took villagers with manual clippers and cow-hide-hard hands weeks to sort the vines for the season. Just squeezing these clippers 2,000 times a day wrecked the upper body. Now three or four people with battery back-packs powering bionic secateurs can do with ease in a week what used to take a month.

Any grubbing-up of old vine stumps attracts small groups of people like seagulls behind a trawler. If you are in the know, you can get there before anyone else, fill your trailer and be off before the hordes descend. These old vines are called *souche* (*suque* in Occitan)* and are a great fuel for log burners, but their real worth is for barbecues. They burn hot with a sweet smell and bequeath a lovely fine, white ash.

In the spring there is not much on the land in the way of stuff to eat, but sometimes it's just as satisfying to know where the best orchid fields are, or where the Bonelli's eagles are nesting, which restaurants are open early. But it's not until summer arrives in late May that things hot up. Then there are traditions such as the procession of each village's animal mascot, and the Fête de la St Pierre in Sête, where the fishermen pay tribute to the sea and to lost sailors by holding a boat-bound jousting tournament. Then in August comes La Feria in Béziers – proper bullfighting, not like that in Magalas. *Death in the Afternoon* stuff.

In the summer there are travelling troupes that go from town to town, village to village, festival to festival, putting on performances in the squares, churches and boulodromes. Most years, one visits Causses and puts on a show in Place Jules Milhau. The square is just the right size to seat 200 or so people, with the stage against the archway into Place de Pompe Neuve and the entrance through Rue des Porches. We have a ringside seat from our dining room. I always go down and get a couple of tickets. One year someone in the queue told the ticket lady that we live in the square. She was surprised I was there and said we didn't have to buy tickets: it was their way of saying thank you for the disruption. But I insisted, and it was kindly remembered. We watch from our balcony like the *seigneur* and *châtelaine*. I don't understand most of what's going

* There's a novel, *Le Loup de la Suque* (named after a hilly area behind the village), by an ex-*maire* of Causses, Didier Douarche, who died in 2013 aged 100. I am working my way through.

on, the more so since sometimes bits are in Occitan. One time, they were saying something I didn't understand, and an actor pointed at us. Whatever he said, the whole crowd thought it hilarious. Someone from the audience shouted, 'N'oubliez pas de Montfort!' and the place erupted in hilarity once again. I thought, what the hell, so I stood, put on a big grin and gave them all the royal wave. Some cheered, a few laughed, most seemed decidedly not amused.

There are film nights up at Le Lézard in the garden, and almost every day there's a roving *dégustation* in one village or another where you pay five or so euros, get a plastic glass on a lanyard and five or six tickets and then you wander around stalls set up by local vineyards exchanging the tickets for a top-up and, if you like it, buying a bottle or two. It's a wonderful way of spending the early evening. If it's really hot, then some villages hang mist sprays from the trees and it's like walking under a rainforest canopy. Make sure you have a designated driver. By seven everyone is utterly pissed.

It is the autumn when Languedoc and the south of France come alive. The holidaymakers have gone home, the days are warm, and there is the hint of woodsmoke in the late-evening air. The autumn is the time of *la vendange*, the grape harvest. Historically this part of the year was regarded as so important that in the French Republican calendar – used for a short while after the Revolution – the month of 22 September to 21 October was named Vendémiaire and designated the first month of the year.

The *vendange* is the time when rural communities come together. There's camaraderie and purpose, hope for a good harvest and optimism for the reward of a year's hard work. The last twelve months of droughts and hailstones, floods, mildew and frosts, *canicules* and maybe even grape rustlers, is all behind them. The *vendange* is the moment when no more can be done, the worrying is past, the harvest will be what it will be.

> Yesterday we picked one last peach from the tree,
> And this morning, in the thick and cool dawn,
> Autumn mist on the neighbouring slopes,
> A fine frost has wrinkled the purple of the grapes.
> Over there do you see the dawn, above the slope?
> The golden vine leaves in the silvery haze?
> The horizon brightens in vague redness,
> And the rising sun leads the grape pickers.*

Tractors are out at all hours, their engines quietly grumbling, headlights shining in the dark hills. The grapes to make white and often rosé are best picked when they are at their coolest in the early hours, when it is said the flavours are most concentrated. You can get a pastis in the middle of the night at Le Helder in Cessenon. The cooperative in Murviel is packed round the clock. Red Alma and blue Braud grape-picking machines straddle the vines, shaking off the bunches, filling tractor trailers full, bouncing along country roads, juice dripping under tailgates. They have a cultural priority on the byways, their grape variety proudly chalked on the back. They'll pull in close to the side to let cars pass, but it's up to you to show your respect. At this time of year everything gives way to the *vendange*. Everywhere smells of Ribena and old sackcloth.

A growing number of vineyards like Mas des Dames now

---

* From 'Les Vendanges' (1860) by Victor de Laprade: Hier on cueillait à l'arbre une dernière pêche, / Et ce matin voici, dans l'aube épaisse et fraîche, / L'automne qui blanchit sur les coteaux voisins. / Un fin givre a ridé la pourpre des raisins. / Là-bas voyez-vous poindre, au bout de la montée, / Les ceps aux feuilles d'or dans la brume argentée ? / L'horizon s'éclaircit en de vagues rougeurs, / Et le soleil levant conduit les vendangeurs.

only pick by hand – the grapes less traumatized – and many are bio as well. At Domaine Des 3 Angles, over in Cazouls-lès-Béziers, Vincent Vabre sings to his vines from his tractor cab.

And when all is safely gathered in, there are parties. If the harvest is good, then all is good cheer. If the harvest is bad, then there is always next year.

Produce festivals are a way of life around Causses. There are chestnut festivals, mimosa festivals, cherry festivals, olive festivals. There are actually truffles from Languedoc, not just from Périgord, and of course there's a truffle festival, in Uzez. Truffles start to form in late April mostly under oak trees and a hundred years ago were common in the countryside. They are now pretty rare due to farming methods and collecting. The big ones can fetch thousands of pounds. Why? Goodness knows, to my mind. They taste sickly rich, the smell too pungent, like dry rot. I find them more than slightly emetic. Francesco Mazzei, the great Italian chef, once served me some tagliatelli with shaved white truffle from Umbria. Literally just tagliatelli coated in butter and then shaved truffle over it. The dish was only served in the autumn when the truffles were available. It cost sixty pounds a plate. Sixty quid. I managed a few mouthfuls, just to be polite.

The days after our meal with Hans and Lotten, the fig tree had become a big thing. There was the slight that we weren't grand enough, trusted enough or local enough to be bestowed with the secret of a fig tree. More fundamental was that there should be a tree that was *the* fig tree. There are hundreds around the village. Some have green figs, some have purple figs. Some are small, others large. Some produce fruits that are pithy inside, some are rich and jammy but small. It hadn't occurred to me that there was a tree that produced the perfect fig: purple, plump and round, soft, thick, sweet and fruity right up to the edge of the skin.

In the evening we roamed the village in our minds. What about that tree by the old cooperative? No, that's got green figs on it. How about the one on the way to the viewpoint just off the track? Maybe, put that on the list. The one on the back road to Fonsalade by the pine trees which have the caterpillar nests on them in the spring? How about that one near the orchid field? Or the one on the road up to Montpeyroux near where the hunting dogs are kennelled? And so it went on. Later, I said, 'How about we follow Hans and Lotten?'

'We can't do that.'

'Why not?'

'Well, it's underhand.'

'We can make it seem like a joke if they see us. I'll get a pipe and a stick-on moustache, and if they see me I'll pretend to be one of the Thompson Twins, and you can pretend to be the other one.'

'They'll let us know soon enough. It must be a Swedish thing. No one in Sweden breaks the rules.'

'What, so they're just joshing with us?'

'Sort of.'

'How about I go down the bar and announce that Hans and Lotten are stripping the secret fig tree? That would sort them out.'

'You're being an arse again. Anyway, it will be too late soon. The season for figs is getting along now, and they will all be either picked or rotten on the ground.'

Another day went by, and still nothing. Then we found ourselves walking along a track through the vineyards, just watching the late-summer butterflies and chatting about this and that. Lola – you'll remember her, our black cocker spaniel – was frolicking about. We rounded a corner, and I turned to see if she was still with us, and she was nowhere to be seen. I shouted and walked back a ways and spotted her in the fields. Her face peeped up, and she romped back, passing what looked like a fig tree I hadn't noticed before. I wandered over. It was nothing to write home about, a bit straggly, a few browning leaves. Then I noticed some black spots on the ground, so walked closer. There they were, the plumpest black figs you'll ever see. 'Kaz, come and look at this,' I shouted.

Standing like two sentinels, we looked up as if the tree were bathed in a celestial beam of godly light and the choir eternal were lifting their voices in rejoices. We pulled some dog poo bags from our pockets and filled them. Not too many, just enough to make perhaps a kilo or two or three of jam and supper for a night or two. When we had finished, there were so many left no one would have known we had been there. We strode purposely back to 1 Place de l'Eglise and snuck in, closing the door behind us. Like Butch and Sundance we emptied our booty onto the table and danced a little jig.

We wanted now to make jam like Lotten's. But there were so many recipes on the interweb we didn't know which one to follow. There was no way we weren't going to do right by these figs, so we had to have the best recipe going. After a couple of hours, we found a really good one. Or one that looked like it would be really good, just quartered figs, brown sugar with a hint of lemon juice and, the kicker, some balsamic vinegar. But we had to be sure, and there was only one way to be sure. But it would be high-risk. We needed Lotten's recipe.

My chum Paul Marshall is a barrister. He's exactly what you would expect from a barrister: ex-army, degrees from LSE and Cambridge. He's only ever had jobs that require dressing up. This is convenient, since he looks great in high boots and a wig. Paul punctuates conversations with 'You're in a minefield there, old chap' and 'I'm not sure that wholly makes sense.' He then asks me questions until I find my arguments on a spike. I know what he's doing but I always get led down a track leading to a dead end of Paul's making. He makes me realize what a woolly thinker I am. What if, I thought, I take a lesson from him in getting to the bottom of the recipe without incriminating myself?

I waited for Lotten to come out and do her daily prune and tidy of the plants on the steps in front of her house.

'*Salut*, Lotten.'

'Hello.'

'Those lemons and peppers are coming on well this year.'

'We've managed to keep them watered. The irrigation system sometimes doesn't work well enough.'

'What do you do with the lemons?'

'Mostly gin and tonic,' she laughed.

'Kaz found some raspberries at SuperU. We thought we would make some jam.'

'Nice,' she said.

'Not sure how much sugar to put in. You make jam, don't you?

'Oh yes, we make a lot of jam in Sweden. Loganberry is very popular. We have it with meatballs.' I'd heard this. They sell it at IKEA. Jam with meatballs. Desperate. She was continuing: 'We would never put jam on toast like you English do. Very odd thing to do with jam. We have jam clubs in Sweden. We pick wild fruits and make all sorts of jams. Actually, raspberry is a favourite. We have it with a butter cookie called Hallongrotta and we have a mixed jam of . . . ' – this was going well – '. . . raspberry and blueberry called Queen's jam. We have jam at *fika*, a tea break, in the afternoon and of course rhubarb jam and . . .'

'Is there a classic recipe for Swedish jam, then?'

'Well, yes.'

'Could you possibly write it down for me?'

'Of course. I'll push it under the door later.'

'Fabulous. Thanks, Lotten.'

I told Kaz and got a double thumbs-up.

So the plan now was to make some fig jam then quietly leave a jar on Hans and Lotten's step and pretend it's from the *Nisse* (Swedish fairies). That would show them not only that we didn't need them to let us into their fig club but also just how fabulously clever and resourceful we are.

About an hour later, a note was pushed under the door. It read as follows:

- 1 kg of fresh fruit
- ½ kg Demerara sugar
- Juice of a lemon
- Multiply as necessary

1. Sterilize your jam jars and lids.
2. Wash the fruit and let dry.
3. Chop the fruit so that it's all about the size of half a thumb and heap into a large stainless-steel pan.
4. Pour on the sugar and the lemon juice, mix gently and leave for 12 hours.
5. Bring to a rolling boil and simmer, stirring occasionally.
6. Use a thermometer. At about 105°C let it simmer until it's 'set'. It should still be runny-ish. It will set properly when it cools in the jars.
7. Write your labels, marking clearly 'Fig Jam, Causses-et-Veyran' and the date.
8. Save two jars for Hans and Lotten.

18

L'Ermitage Saint-Etienne

Visigoths – randonnée etiquette – top of the world –
Schnauzer – incarnate red – a short service – Field of the
Cloth of Gold – Le cambrioleur de chat!

Every year at Pentecost, there is a penitent *randonnée* to the
Visigoth L'Ermitage Saint-Etienne on top of a peak near the
village of Saint-Nazaire-de-Ladarez about 5 kilometres from
Causses. To get there you take the D19 north and instead of
hanging a left to Cessenon and Roquebrun carry straight on
past the Falaise du Landeyran, where there's a good quartzite 3
to 7c climbing wall with permanent anchors for weekenders,
and on to the sign for Domaine des Madalle. The air always
seems a little damp after this point and colder. As you round the
next corner, you may get the same feeling I do, that of passing
through a hazy time slip to a previous century. The valley cliffs
close in on both sides, with the Ruisseau de Landeyran on your
right, and the first thing you pass as you get to the outskirts of
the village is the cemetery. I never look back from this point. I
worry that the road will have faded into grass and forest.

Saint-Nazaire-de-Ladarez is a little smaller than Causses,
dominated by the huge church in the centre. We don't really
know any of the French people in Saint-Nazaire. I always get
the feeling they are looking at me as if I had just walked into
the Slaughtered Lamb. But we do have a number of friends
who have small houses in the village. Swedes naturally, Outi
and Magnus, a wonderful Boston couple, Jennifer and Kevin,

whose children are unfairly talented musicians, and James and Clive. James was a flight attendant with British Airways for thirty years and is one of the driest, funniest storytellers you could meet. Clive is a former primary school deputy head-teacher who has more than a little of Melvyn Hayes about him. James has the most extraordinary Barbie collection. He doesn't keep them in France but brings a couple each visit to decorate the living room. One I best remember was of a Pan Am air hostess from the 1960s. The doll is the doll, but the clothes are exquisite, down to perfect tiny Pan Am hat, jacket and bag.

Saint-Nazaire is where Causses' hirsute, round butcher lived. He had a small restaurant here, famed for its boiled pigs' feet. We went a couple of times and met his wife, who was lovely, spoke pretty perfect English and handled front of house. But all was not what it seemed. We learned that he was violent towards her. I'm not sure what happened to him after this came out. Certainly he was ostracized. His shop in Causses closed, as did the restaurant and the *traiteur* business. I never saw him again after that.

Just outside the village on the Causses side is a twisting road which in parts is almost vertical, leading to a path winding through the woods to L'Ermitage Saint-Etienne. You can see it from the top of Montpeyroux behind Causses. It's a real eyrie. Each year, on the seventh Sunday after Easter, the villagers of Saint-Nazaire and anyone else who cares to join them trek to the hermitage.

We were told to arrive with some water and coffee and whatever else we liked to drink and, if we wanted some lunch, a sandwich or two, since the walk was arranged so that by the time we reached the top it would be lunchtime. We weren't listening properly. Kaz probably was, but as usual I wasn't. She probably asked if I wanted to take something, and I said no to something I wasn't listening to, and that's how we ended up with a small bag with a bottle of water and a couple of biscuits.

By the time we arrived in the square at Saint-Nazaire just before 10 a.m. there were about fifty or sixty people milling around. I recognized a few from the Causses walking group – Mondays at 9 a.m. in the late autumn, winter and early spring; start location passed along by tom-toms. We *bonjour* them and *ça va* them, and they welcome us congenially.

And then we set off.

Randonnées, hikes, are a big social thing. Chatting is expected and required. But in French only. After one of my first Causses club walks I was thoroughly ticked off by way of a handwritten note for talking in English to a Scottish chap who had just arrived in the village – I was only trying to make him feel welcome. The thing was, I was ticked off not by one of the French but by one of the English. There are none so pitiless as the proselytized. I've met a number of English who want to be more French than the French. Once I actually over-heard an English woman in Pézenas correct a waiter's grammar to show off to her chums. Now, there are any number of reasons why this is not a good idea. Even if you don't mind being regarded as a prat, a *serveur* is the last person you should patronize, since in all likelihood your lunch will arrive garnished with saliva and fag ash.

We troop out of the village and take a steep side-road to the right. The weather is spectacular, warm and promising to get hot, the light is mellow, and the breeze is full. There is a pathway from the centre of the village, but on this day we go by the road route, since there are so many of us. The walk is not far, 3 or 4 kilometres tops – hardly a *randonnée*. The Causses hikers think nothing of 15 kilometres in a long morning, and most of the participants are well over seventy. But the walk to the hermitage is as close to vertical as it gets. Well, in my mind, at any rate. Pretty soon, I'm panting, and our band of walkers is striding ahead, many using skiing-type walking poles, which seem to make them glide effortlessly uphill like an optical illusion. Now and again a car squeezes by on the thin road. As they pass, I glimpse some very elderly people inside.

I think I've mentioned before that 1 Place de l'Eglise is built on a Visigoth graveyard, so Causses would have been occupied when the hermitage was built. Unlike the Romans, who left a big galumphing footprint on the area, the Visigoths left very little. By AD 500 or so they had effectively taken over from the Romans a great swathe of what is now the middle of Spain and Portugal, north past Bordeaux to around La Rochelle and Nantes, inland to around Clermont-Ferrand and then south along the Languedoc and Provençal coast to the border of Italy. It was all governed from Toulouse. L'Ermitage Saint-Etienne is a rare survivor. It dates from at least the seventh century and is probably older. Named for Saint Stephen, who was one of the seven deacons appointed by Jesus' apostles to look after the poor as a bit of a sop to the Greek-speaking Jews, who were feeling left out. The story goes he drew too much attention to himself, performing miracles and becoming a terrific preacher, which didn't endear him to the Sanhedrin, the Jewish supreme court, who dragged him along for a scolding. He saw them off as well. He may have been a terrific debater but he plainly couldn't judge a room. The Sanhedrin took umbrage and had him promptly stoned to death. He was a little overlooked as a martyr until AD 415, exactly the time the Visigoths were in the ascendant in France and Spain, when a priest called Lucian dreamed of where he was killed, and on 26 December of that year ('on the feast of Stephen'), his bones were found and taken to Jerusalem and interred.

The road up the mountain is carved through the *garrigue* and winds back and forth to reduce the gradient, but it's still a long haul. After a couple of hours or so we reach a flatter part, and half a kilometre further, there's a wooden sign pointing into what looks like dense woodland. We can see people disappearing into the trees, so we follow. Then it's upwards on a track of hard earth and scattered stone punctuated by boulders, and steep scrambles, scrapping past scrubby oak, until after 300 metres or so we pop out into sunlight, and above us is the stone hermitage. We scrabble and heave the last few metres, legs like jelly, and suddenly there we are. Top of the world.

The view is breathtaking. In front are the peaks of the Pyrenees, to the left the sparkling blue Mediterranean, to the right the Montagne Noire creasing the land right up to the Auvergne, and behind me is the biggest black Giant Schnauzer I have ever seen. This fellow is huge, for a Schnauzer at any rate. With his docked tail and shiny coat like wet coal he is the very model of a top dog Schnauzer. I wish I could remember his name or to whom he belonged. I do remember him being perfectly at home. He popped over for a brief sniff and *salut* and then back to business, just poking around. I get a hint that his little stub of a tail is wagging, but who knows? A minute or two later, he rejoins me on a rocky ledge. The two of us on the brink of nothing much at all, except air and gravity, down perhaps 200 or 300 metres. I point out to him the abandoned marble quarry in the valley, the rusty crane in among the slabs which hadn't quite made it out before the last whistle blew fifty years ago. He seems interested. 'If you were to tell your chums over your Royal Canin supper this evening that you have seen one of only three or four Languedoc red marble quarries ever excavated, I'm sure they would be impressed. The marble extracted down there is unique, called 'Incarnate Red'. Languedoc was famous for

this unique marble, which ranges in colour from deep orange to almost crimson with white veins running through it. Really beautiful, if a little bling.' I look down, and my friend is plainly not into the history of marble. I try and impress with a last hurrah. 'In the seventeenth century it caught the eye of Louis XIV, who used it extensively in Versailles. You'll find a few Incarnate Red marble fireplaces in Causses.' But Mr Schnauzer is now completely over the history of marble and has progressed to chewing his arse.

People are moving into the chapel for a service, and I join Kaz in the queue. I hadn't noticed before, but there is a priest among us who has put on his white vestments and set up behind a table at the far end away from the door with a simple cross placed upon it. The chapel is tiny, no more than 10 metres from end to end and 3 or so metres wide under a low barrel roof almost identical to the *cave* at 1 Place de l'Eglise, though the window slits here are punched through instead of curved in. As with our *cave*, the inside walls are lime painted probably a hundred plus years ago and are now flaking and crumbling. The thing that lingers is how cool it is and dark. Two small slit windows let in beams of bright white sunshine and a pool of light from the doorway. Those inside are a mixed bunch of old, middle-aged and children. I'm not sure how many are from Saint-Nazaire or indeed who are French and who are not. It reminds me of the short story called 'Let's Go to Golgotha' by Garry Kilworth, where time-travelling tourists are warned that they must follow the historical events and chant for Barabbas. One of the time travellers loses his way and realizes that there are no actual people from AD 33 in the square, they are all time-travelling tourists.

The service is short, and we all file back outside, where those who couldn't get in are now starting to make their way back down the slope. It's well into lunchtime, and my laissez-faire attitude is now coming back to haunt me. I look inside my backpack to see the pitiful sight of a bottle of water and a biscuit or two. I vow never again to go anywhere without a full three-course lunch.

As we stagger down the slope, people are happy and talking. The lady in front tackles me.

'*Tu es anglais. Es-tu en vacances?*' (There's a good deal of 'tu'-ing to strangers in Languedoc.)

'*Non, nous avons une maison dans Causses.*'

'*Nous venons du nord de Bédareaux. Est-ce que Causses est proche?*'

'*Oui, le village suivant. Une journée si merveilleuse, le ciel est tout simplement merveilleux.*'

'*Es-tu déjà venu ici avant?*'

'*Non, c'est vraiment génial. Nous allons revenir ici. Je pense qu'il y a un chemin à travers le village.*'

As we burst out of the wood, it's like the Field of the Cloth of Gold. In the clearing and all along the road are tents and tables, cars and caravans. Food is being passed hand to hand in cold boxes to tables already laid. Bottles of wine are being walked from one pitch to the next with a slap on the back, a glimpse at the label and a smile and a thanks. A minivan pulls up and decants people so old they have shrunk almost into a ball. Barbecues are firing up with a communal trailer of *souche* up for grabs. I spot Clive and James and René and Brigitte Thiltges from atelier 'Les Arts du Jardin', who waves *salut*. My old friend the black Schnauzer is romping towards me, followed by a group of whooping children. He scoots past my legs, does a hand-break turn and is off back again.

We, however, walk solemnly on down the road, the weight of the water and biscuits heavy in my backpack. As we pass the middle few tents an old lady shouts to us, '*Messieurs-dames, vous ne restez pas?*' It is one of my old ladies from the church.

'*Bonjour, madame. Désolé nous n'avons pas de déjeuner.*'

'*Mais bien sûr. Vous avez une place ici!*'

We do the English thing and say thank you for inviting us but we couldn't possibly intrude. But by then she is on her feet and has Kaz and me by the shoulders, the rest of their table, numbering probably fifteen, are on their feet, and chairs are being shuffled and places laid, and a huge fellow whom I had never seen before is pumping my hand. '*Enchanté! L'attrape-chat!*'

19

Christmas

Earth stood hard as iron – the art of the wood-burning
stove – Mass at Murviel – Monsieur le Maire et le Conseil
Municipal – La soirée

Christmas in an unheated twelfth-century *maison de mur* in rural France is cold. 'Earth stood hard as iron' doesn't come close. Winter in an unheated stone house in the south of France is a whole different sort of domestic cold. It's the sort of cold that gets into your bones and won't let go. It's when you have a roaring log fire and when you turn your face away you can still see your breath. Four jumpers make no difference. The walls radiate cold. Climbing into bed means with all your clothes on to be progressively peeled as you warm. It's waking up in the middle of the night with your nose frozen so that you have to sleep with your face under the covers. It's ice on the inside of the windows. I imagine what it was like when this was the norm for centuries. The past is indeed another very cold country.

That first year we decided Noël en France would be an adventure and arrived in Causses on 21 December. The drive down had been unusual. Paris was packed, and as we came past Clermont-Ferrand it had begun to snow. When we arrived, it was dark, and the temperature was -4.

Early on, all we had to heat 1 Place de l'Eglise were two very handsome wood-burning stoves, a big one in the living room and a smaller one in our bedroom upstairs. But there was a problem. It was six o'clock in the evening, and we had no wood. We did the only thing we could do. We cold-footed it to the Excalibur restaurant in Magalas, stuffed ourselves with pizza and heat and rushed back to pile into bed fully clothed and wait the night out.

In the morning, I peeped from under a doughy mass of duvet and blanket. It felt like I was turfed in. It was dark, but I could glimpse grey light beyond the shutters. A decision had to be made: to remain warm or get up for a pee.

I hadn't found myself in this exact position since I was six, when we lived in a draughty bungalow called 'Sandbanks' at the top of a potholed drive in Lichfield, Staffordshire. It was the winter of 1963, one of the three or four worst of the twentieth century, when 'Love Me Do' was the first song that got into my head, still yet to become the song of a generation. The excitements for a six-year-old in a perpetual snowy winter were unending. The canal down the road froze over. Piles of grit and sand on every corner demanded to be jumped into before it was flung under skidding tyres. I loved the way mud got oily during the day then froze solid overnight. Snow fell and went grey but didn't disappear. In the evenings I watched ice crystals creep and cover windows like the Andromeda Strain.

Our family decamped into the kitchen, where a stove roared. We had a black-and-white Bush television in the corner continually playing newsreels of cars stuck in snowdrifts, helicopters dropping bales of hay to scurrying sheep and trains blowing white fountains as they sped through white countryside. We seemed to hibernate in that room. It was damp and warm and full of the smells of soap and coal and cooking. Baths were taken fast in clammy steam that condensed and ran down the walls. Out of the kitchen, away from the bathroom, the cold was dry and hard. It wrinkled up my face as I ran from hot kitchen to cold hallway to cold room, curling up in cold bed nested under blankets. Outside, the air pinched, and each morning we would climb into the Austin in the hope that it would chug and start. Most mornings it didn't, and we would run and slide for a bus that skidded and puffed up the hill to St Michael's school.

The boys' toilets were open urinals with a rudimentary lean-to roof. That winter, they were always full of snow. We competed to melt the most ice. The pipes were lagged with rags but invariably frozen. Icicles hung like lances from every ledge. At least at school there was the comfort of huge cast-iron radiators as warm as red-hot coal. We would struggle to see who could sit on them the longest, until one boy, with true grit, scalded his arse.

My bladder demanded a decision. I crawled out, wrapped myself in a coat left by the side of the bed, slipped on my shoes and made for the bathroom.

Today's task was assessing the fuel and wood situation before we were forced to start burning the furniture. The nearest place where there might be some logs was SuperU at Murviel. This was good news. It meant that I had to use the car, which had a heater, and heated seats. Sometimes in summer when it just got too hot we might sit in the car and cool ourselves with the aircon. I know AC is not PC, but needs must.

I managed to get a couple of bags of small logs and some kindling in those orange plastic string bags for an extortionate amount of money and got back before anyone was up. I wanted to surprise them with a roaring log fire and breakfast. I opened the log burner with great hope and fogged breath. I had been a boy scout, so this was going to be not only a doddle but a trip down memory lane to the days when, each week, after dib-dib-dobbing, strange middle-aged men placed their hands on my shoulder and squeezed just a little too hard.

In a twinkling, the fire blazed. I piled on the logs. A beacon had been lit. A signal that good times were just around the corner. The kettle went on – a figure of speech. Bread went under the grill. Smashing. In the six minutes it took to get breakfast underway and return to the wood burner to inspect the comforting flames, all that remained of the two sacks of logs was a pile of red embers. The outside of the burner was merely warm, the room silent and cold and grey.

By mid-morning, a council of war had been convened. George and Freya were open to two solutions. One, we get in the car and drive home. Two, we get in the car and drive to the nearest hotel. We were hardier than that, I said. Ideas for heat were solicited. Jogging round the room was mooted to little amusement. As an immediate palliative we decided to turn on all the gas rings. All that did was make faces hot and red, as the air heated up and made the place feel like one gigantic lukewarm oven. The obvious answer was to go buy a heater. Something had to be done, and the credit card was sparkling in the air like one of those spinning coin rewards you get in video games.

The solution was something you don't often see in Anglo-Saxon countries. A 'computerized' paraffin heater. People of a certain age remember those upright grey Valor heaters where the front is hooked off to reveal a chimney with a little window in the bottom. You turn the chimney a half-turn anticlockwise to reveal a big round wick which you light; then you stick the chimney back quick, adjust the wick so it glows blue, and away you go. They were dangerous, smelly and gave out not much heat. But in the days before ubiquitous central heating, they were really common.

The French ones are like SpaceX in comparison. I spent the cost of a small second-hand car on something called a Zibro Sre25tc. You fill a cartridge with kerosene, pop it in, press a button, set the temperature, and that's it. It was a miracle.

Within five minutes the room was toasty. The mood changed. A Christmas tree was bought. Lunch was a feast, and decorations appeared from nowhere. Food and heat. We were rock-and-rolling. It took about five days before the walls were not like permafrost.

Christmas in France is different from the Anglo-Saxon version. Presents are opened on Christmas Eve/early hours of Christmas Day after a very elaborate and regimented dinner called Réveillon. This starts after Midnight Mass and goes on into the early hours of Christmas Day. In Languedoc, Réveillon goes as follows:

- Definitely oysters from the Étang de Thau.
- Possibly lobster.
- Maybe foie gras and snails and scallops.
- Definitely a main course of roast turkey with chestnut stuffing – chestnuts are a big thing in the Languedoc.
- Perhaps guinea fowl or quail or pheasant or goose.
- Cheese might follow.
- Thirteen desserts – popular in Provence and leaking into Languedoc festivities – a cornucopia of nuts and fruit and a cake called *pompe à l'huile*.
- Finally, and most definitely, a Languedoc must-have, is the *bûche de Nöel* – a chocolate yule log.

All this was for the future, as we didn't have a clue then what was what. We were, however, tipped off about Murviel Midnight Mass starting at 11 p.m. Welcoming the Christ Child is one thing. A heated church is another. We set off around ten to get in early, but that, it appeared, was late. So many people were making for the church of St John the Baptist up on the hill that we had to park outside the village. A jolly mood was in the air. The stars were out and a frost was sparkling on stone and leaf alike. We walked with the throng and joined a bustle of people around the church door until the crowd momentum popped us through into another place. It was warm. Warm. Not hot or cold, but warm. The amber light from the hundreds of candles was the colour of warm. It smelled of warm incense and soap. The place was packed with excited, smiling people, greeting and chatting, clustering around a huge, almost life-size nativity. There was no room in the nave, so we were ushered up into the organ loft and perched in a perfect position.

I wish I could remember the service. I wish I could bring that hour to you as it was for me. I am not religious, but in that church at that moment few places I have ever been were more warm and peaceful.

On the evening of New Year's Day, Causses throws a party. The whole village turns out for a cross between the summer Fête and an annual general meeting. It gives the *maire* and his deputies the opportunity to be applauded for their work, and for the *maire* himself to give a round-up of the year in Causses and the state of the finances. It's a must-have ticket at Salle Jules Milhau. There's free wine and food and above all a cabaret.

On entry you grab your glass and a few nibbles and find yourself a seat. We shuffle to a couple of chairs in among the old ladies, who welcome us with wide smiles and chatter.

We all settle down for the show. On comes the great Monsieur Baro, accompanied by much cheering and the occasional heckle from the floor. He speaks about the year and about the new building works around the village, the *vendange*, the compensation for the vines destroyed by wind or rain or hailstones. He then goes through the village finances, by which time half the audience are either on their way to the bar or coming back from the bar or talking to a neighbour across the way. Children have already gone rogue, sliding under seats and being shouted at by their parents. Then the *maire's* deputies are introduced, and they troop up, a little embarrassed, form a semicircle, and, as their names are read out, they are cursorily applauded. By now, everyone has had enough and just want the cabaret to begin. Suddenly, the lights dim, music strikes up, and everyone settles.

It's a jazz funeral march much like the beginning of the Bond film *Live and Let Die*. A spotlight illuminates a dark, hooded, cloaked figure who slowly appears from stage right. After three steps, another figure exactly the same reveals itself, then another and another. The quartet turns to face the audience. The music stops. For three or four long seconds, there's silence. Suddenly, the band bursts into a gospel belter, spotlights flood the stage, and the foursome throw up their heads, cast off their cloaks in one grand, snappy, dramatic, coordinated movement, revealing four girls in black stockings and suspenders, red feather boas, plumed head-dresses and red satin nipple tassels. The place goes crazy. Every chap old or young suddenly seems to have a camera. The girls on stage are dancing like it's Studio 54. One of them takes her red boa, finds the *maire*, loops it around his neck and leads him back into the spotlights, gyrating all the while. The place goes apoplectic. The children are now at the front by the stage, dancing along. Then on comes Céline Dubois et ses Danseurs – it's as close as Causses will ever get to the Moulin Rouge.

What a night. For an hour the stage is alight with colour and dancers and singers, and the crowd is as one. By the end, everyone is exhausted and supremely happy. This is the proper way to spend the European grant.

Not late, we drift into the freezing night as the stars shine and the laughter soars. We shout valedictions in French and English, link arms and wander the quiet streets, the moon lighting our way.

20

Thyme and Lavender

*Pachamunu – hardly a breath – palimpsest – locking up
and going home – repaired with gold*

If peradventure, Reader, it has been thy lot to waste the
golden years of thy life – thy shining youth – in the irksome
confinement of an office; to have thy prison days prolonged
through middle age down to decrepitude and silver hairs,
without hope of release or respite; to have lived to forget that
there are such things as holidays, or to remember them but
as the prerogatives of childhood; then, and then only, will
you be able to appreciate my deliverance.

Charles Lamb, 'The Superannuated Man',
Essays of Elia, 1833

Scratched on the lintel above the front door of 1 Place de
l'Eglise is the date 1782. Every time I walk up to the door and
place the key in the lock, I look up and imagine someone, his
feet planted exactly where mine are, scratching away above his
head. It couldn't have taken more than a minute or two. I say
'his', since it would almost certainly have been a 'he'. I cannot
imagine a woman from that time taking it upon herself to do
it, though who knows. He must have been numerate – or he
asked someone who was numerate – to either to do it for him
or show him how: 1782 was a time when two-thirds of people
in France could neither read nor write. But that's not to say that

there were not scholars and writers in the smallest of villages. Jacques Vanière, the celebrated Jesuit and modern Latin poet, was born in 1664 literally a stone's throw from 1 Place de l'Eglise and died there in 1739. His birth is commemorated by a plaque among the tiny group of houses in a square named after him.

The person who scratched the date above the door was plainly proud of where he lived or was marking a moment. He couldn't afford a plaque or a stone mason so he did it himself. Stepped back, kissed his wife on the cheek and smiled at their life to come or their life passed. At least that's one of the many scenes I play out. As he admired his handiwork, Louis XVI had been on the French throne for seven years. In Avignon, just 140 kilometres or so east, brothers Joseph-Michel and Jacques-Étienne Montgolfier lost control of their first prototype hot-air balloon, watched it float off and then crash-land two kilometres away, nearly killing a passerby. Across the Atlantic, the British admiral Sir George Rodney defeated the French Fleet at the Battle of Saintes, paving the way for the peace treaty of Paris. And our man stepped in to 1 Place de l'Eglise for his supper.

There are hints all over the house of previous lives. We tried to retain everything we could as we made it habitable and comfortable. The chute from the roof down through the house to the stone trough in the *cave* we left open. It's on the terrace now with a glass top and a light from below so you can see right down to the *cave*. It's a talking point, but it's also a time tunnel. The *pigeonnier* is gone. We simply couldn't save it. The acid guano had turned every piece of wood to sponge, and we didn't have the money to rebuild it. It's a shame. It might have made a great little observatory if we had popped the roof and installed a telescope.

One winter the temperature didn't rise above freezing for nearly a month and everything froze. Like an idiot I forgot to turn off the water mains – you can be sure I do that religiously now – and the pipe on the roof burst, spraying water over the roof terrace, creating a berg a foot thick. It topped the tanking and started to melt from the bottom, leaking down the wall through the house all the way to the bottom. Thank goodness our friend Joe had a key and came and had a look and found it before the whole inside of the house fell in. He switched off the water and shovelled the ice out of the hay door into the square. There's a photo of it looking like a New York sidewalk after a snowstorm. We were lucky. Other ice-bound houses didn't get noticed until the thaw. The first sign was water gushing into the street under front doors.

The *cave* was always a project and is still ongoing. A couple of years ago we managed to persuade Jason, a lovely Irish chap who lives in the village and does all sorts of things to make ends meet, including customized art for classic cars, spent a week barrowing out about six tons of rubble, the accumulation of a century. Sadly, nothing of note was unearthed other than the bedrock about two metres lower than the outside street. And there appears to be a spring of some sort in one corner, which bubbles up when there's lots of rain and partially floods the place.

Charles, the estate agent, told me all those years ago that the house was once the Mairie, and at another time the school, and it was undoubtedly two houses at some point centuries past. Imagine all those people who have lived here over that time. Not always happy. Not always kind. Not always the recipient of kindness. Maybe cruel or worse. But also, hopefully, among those lives, lives well lived.

Sixteen years we have been at 1 Place de l'Eglise. Hardly a breath in its millennium of life. It's sometimes a little difficult to remember what the house looked like the day I walked in with Charles. I'm told he still lives around and about, still working for Freddy. Some say separated from his wife Sophie, others that they are still together. I guess his daughter would be sixteen or seventeen now. I pass the Pachamunu café, where we first met, from time to time. It's now called Le Grand Café, and I've not been in since it changed hands a few years ago. I'm sure it's great but, well, it's not the Pachamunu.

Walk into 1 Place de l'Eglise now, and there's no trace of the old stove with the nut-brown flue driving up into the scorched ceiling. The floor is all nicely tiled, the fireplace remade, and the walls white and clean. Where once hops and old bottles jostled under the wasps' nest is François's dapper kitchen. There is no fertilizer bag stuffing up the window. Madame Petit's bedroom is now Freya's. In summer, the tall window is always open, the breeze puffs out blanched linen curtains above a small mustard-coloured sofa much used for reading. This is Freya's bedroom but it is a reading room. Freya is a passionate reader. In this room she walks in others' shoes: Getas and Padukas, Moccasins and Pattens, Chopines and Pointinini, Poulaines, Pampooties and Sabots, Stilettos and Mary Janes, Oxfords and Brogues, Jellys, and Ruby Slippers. Lives real and imagined, inseparable.

Where once Madame de France led the revolution, there is now a poster of *Tintin and Red Rackham's Treasure*. Where once there was the dressing room there is now a bathroom. Above the bed is a print of Picasso's *Dove of Peace*. Like all houses, 1 Place de l'Eglise is a palimpsest. Our iteration will soon blur and then be gone but something of us, however intangible, will, I like to think, remain.

When France was shut in 2020 because of Covid-19, I sent a couple of meals' worth of money to Rik. When we managed to travel in late summer, we went for dinner and he greeted me warmly, thanked me and demanded I come see where my euros had gone. There in the garden was a splendid new outside toilet he had built himself for the garden diners. It is terrific. And the flush is super-hygienic. You just wave your hand over it, and away it goes. I was impressed. 'You paid for that,' he exclaimed proudly. 'Your contribution paid for the fancy flush.' He shook my hand. 'Now let me get you supper.'

What with work, for over a decade, I spent perhaps three or four weeks each year at 1 Place de l'Eglise. Kaz spent the summer, and I would come back for a weekend every so often. Over the hot summer days, she would gently bed in, relax, slow down. She got to know people I didn't know who greeted her warmly. Me introduced as 'my husband'. I became more of an outsider as I watched her French become better and better as mine stood still. I became an observer.

We got WiFi only recently. For those years, Kaz would wander down to the bar to use theirs. René would serve her coffee and buttery sacristain, and she would do her emails. I'd drive over to Carcassonne to get Risible Ryanair back to Stansted. Those days were hard.

At the end of the summer, I would travel down for a week or so and then drive us back. We would fuss over the place, leaving it as we would want to find it when we returned. Wandering from room to room, glimpsing memories in every nook and corner.

As the sun rose, we would pack the car and make our way towards Murviel, then Béziers, Clermont-Ferrand, Paris and London. As we depart, we open the car windows to breathe in the last redolence of thyme and lavender and the peaceful smell of warmth.

When I am in London I daydream. I imagine myself a spectre in the night on the roof terrace below the black adzed beams, in drizzly rain or below the stars, and I imagine 1,000 years of lost stories.

But there is one last story which is not lost. It is a story I find very difficult to tell.

George.

Who loved the sun; who bathed with me in the cool water of the River Orb; who chatted about things he wanted to know more of; who walked with me in the silence of the mountains; who loved Le Lézard Bleu on balmy evenings; who lounged on the terrace; who sat and listened to the breeze on his favourite bench under the pine tree overlooking the valley, died in the late evening of 22 March 2018, two weeks after his twenty-eighth birthday.

George's room at 1 Place de l'Eglise is now my study. It's still George's room and always will be until the house becomes someone else's, and then it will become part of their story. I am writing this now at my desk with George's bed behind me. During the day, I sometimes hear a puff of breeze from a window and for half a second I think it's him. I see someone in the square and double-take. I hear someone laugh, and for a twinkle of a moment I simply know he's there.

Sometimes, reality bursts through as if I've been plugged into the mains. The shock ebbs, I am numb and then I return. When he died it was like ink had been dropped into a glass of spring water. At the beginning all I could see was the black drop as it looped and curled as it spread, slowly greying my life forever. For a long while, I continually tripped over whys. But eventually I realized that whys only lead to more whys.

In the dark days soon after George's funeral, a beautiful Japanese pot came up for auction in the Far East. I was intrigued. Not because it was estimated at hundreds of thousands of pounds – that seems common now in international auctions. I was intrigued because it was broken. By the time 1 Place de l'Eglise was 300 years old, half the world away a Japanese Shogun named Ashikagi Yoshimasa dropped his best tea bowl. He obviously loved that bowl. I imagine his pain as he held the shards in his hand. But he was not about to give up on his prized possession, so he sent it away for repair, and by and by it was returned. To his horror it was clamped back together with ugly, grey, metal staples. He was heartbroken and demanded his artisans find a more beautiful way of repairing it. Over the next hundred years the art of Kintsugi was born, mixing tree resin with gold dust, making not just a mend but something exquisite, something which does not try and bring back the original but celebrates its history.

Time for me is divided into whole and broken. When George was in the world and when he is not. Sometime in the future I might stop thinking, on a certain day George did this or that. Perhaps there will be a moment he will go on his way. I will not make any more memories of George, but what memories I have, what adventures we had, what laughs we had, what trials we had.

Those who have travelled this same road will know that there is little comfort to be found. But I know we have been lucky to have shared contentment with George at 1 Place de l'Eglise.

Epilogue

Michel, who must now be in his seventies or eighties, can be seen almost every day in summer, sitting in his shorts and T-shirt on a kitchen chair at the side of Rue de la République. He is fit and buff. When cars pass, he looks up for a moment and then goes back to his book. I always wonder what he's reading.

Along the back lane to the viewpoint overlooking the valley on the way to Cabriole past the house we call the Hacienda is the stone garden that Michel built. It's very securely fenced but not private as such; the fence is there, I think, to frame it. Inside is a medley of stone constructions. A bothy. Beautiful stone walls. A stone shelter with a stone table. Benches of stone. Picassoesque welded sculptures are dotted among olive trees, which are laid out just so. Everything is just so: tidy and smart with small, well-tended shrubs and yuccas, the ground gravelled with broken stone, raked and weeded. Everything is perfect. There doesn't seem to be mortar between the stones. I imagine the hard physical work, the concentration, the careful arrangement. I've never seen Michel there. I've never seen him or anyone there in sixteen years. I wonder if Michel built it as a sign of defiance or as a memorialization. Whatever. There it is. Just a stone sign announcing that this is Las Airos: in Occitan, the place of the wind, the place where the wind winnows, the place where that which is important is separated from that which is not.

Some evenings, after dinner, we take a wander past Las Airos along the dusty track a few hundred metres to the bench under a Scots pine facing the valley across to Fonsalade, Mont Peyroux and the Montagne Noire. Through the year, the view is like a less frenetic Pieter Breughel, so many trades one after the other busy in the vineyards below.

We sit quietly, like attentive guests, watching the sun dawdle from yellow to orange to deep, rippling cinnabar. As darkness falls, a breeze patters up the valley, rustling pine needles above our heads. Slowly the constellations and planets appear. Before it is dark enough to make us stumble on the path, we stand, and Lola creaks as she stretches first her front paws then her back, shakes and makes it plain it's time for the five of us to wander hopefully, home.

Acknowledgements

Without the following this book would not have been written. It is their fault and theirs alone.

Dan Bunyard: my Max Perkins.

Tim and Margaret Cave: fellow nemophilists.

John Andrews: the polymath of Causses.

Lola: the dog of happiness.

Hans and Lotten Bjerke: *skål!*

My Mum.

Gail Blackhall: the doyenne of the misplaced modifier.

Ellie Hughes and Beatrix McIntyre: providers of help and advice. Free to those that can afford it, very expensive to those that can't.

Most importantly the Caussanais, the people of Causses-et-Veyran, especially, in no particular order: Claude, Patrick and Dani, René and Bridgette, Michel Bonnafous, Sébastian, Monsieur Baro, Julie, René and Patricia, Fanny and Benoit, and Merlin and Valentine, Liz and John, Sue, Christine and Andrew, John and Penny, Simon and Sarah, Annie and Clare. And salut to Rik Kat, more than an innkeeper.

But above all to my darling daughter Freya. What an amazing person you are. And of course to Kaz, my soul mate.

Finally, for the moment at any rate, from the great Michel de Montaigne:

'All moral philosophy can be applied to a common and private life, just as one with a richer composition. Each man carries the entire form of the human condition . . . A learned man is not learned in all things: but a sufficient man is sufficient throughout, even to ignorance itself; here my book and I go hand in hand together.' (*Essays*, Chapter II, 'Of Repentance')